medicare 2

I have Medicare Part A & B, now what?

case publications

table of contents

introduction

Thank you for purchasing this book. Whether you found it through a referral, a search, or just by chance — I'm truly grateful you picked it up. No matter where you live in the country, my hope is that what's inside gives you the clarity and direction you've been looking for.

Because for me, this work didn't start in a classroom or an office — it started at my own kitchen table, with my mom.

When my mom turned 65, I wasn't a broker yet. But because she didn't fully understand how the Medicare system worked, she turned to me for help.

I've always been good at problem-solving, so I dove in. I spent weeks buried in Google searches, watching endless YouTube videos, sitting on three-way calls with Medicare, and calling carriers directly — all while walking my mom through every piece of the puzzle. Eventually, it clicked. I figured it out. And more importantly, I was able to explain it to her in plain English — start to finish.

Oddly enough, once my mom understood it all, she started sending her friends my way. They were in the exact same boat: confused, overwhelmed, and unsure who to trust. I wasn't licensed yet, but I found myself genuinely enjoying the process — breaking things down, solving problems, and helping people feel more confident.

So, I made it official. I applied to agencies, got licensed, and began helping people professionally. Fast forward to today, and I've helped thousands of clients across a wide range of situations — and I've written this book to reach even more.

This book isn't for people who are just starting out with Medicare. It's for people who've already enrolled in Parts A and B — but now find themselves stuck in the fog of "what comes next."

You already took that first step, but no one told you how many choices were waiting for you after the enrollment card arrived. Should you go with a Medicare Advantage plan or pair Original Medicare with a Medigap plan and Part D drug coverage? Should you stick with the employer coverage your HR department offered? What happens if you choose wrong? Will it lock you into something long-term? Will you still be able to see your doctors?

And what if you're a veteran, a military retiree, or someone with access to VA, TRICARE, or CHAMPVA — do those benefits change the equation?

This book is for people who already took that first Medicare step, but now feel like they're lost in the middle of something no one explained clearly. Maybe you're 65 and just retired. Maybe you're 68 and still working part-time. Maybe you have an employer plan but aren't sure if it's still the best fit. Or maybe you picked something last year and now you're second-guessing.

If that sounds like you, you're exactly who this book was written for — someone who followed the rules but still doesn't feel fully settled in your decision.

But if you haven't yet enrolled in Medicare — if you're still approaching that first big step — then I recommend starting with my first book, *Medicare 1: Starting Your Medicare Journey*, which is already available on Amazon. That book lays the foundation for how Medicare works and how to enroll the right way from the beginning. This second book builds on that groundwork and helps you move forward with confidence.

I wrote this because I've sat across the table from people like you. I've seen how hard it is to get straight answers. I've seen how quickly people get pulled into plans that don't match their needs — not because they made bad choices, but because they didn't know what to ask. And most importantly, I've seen how powerful it is when someone finally understands their options and gets to make a decision with clarity, not fear.

As a broker licensed in multiple states — and someone based right here in New Jersey — I've had the privilege of helping thousands of people navigate this system. I've sat across kitchen tables, answered late-night phone calls, and reviewed coverage for people with every kind of health and financial situation. I've helped clients fix mistakes they didn't know they made — and I've helped others avoid them entirely. This book is a reflection of everything I've learned from walking beside real people as they made some of the most important coverage decisions of their lives.

Throughout this book, I've included tools to help you make confident decisions. You'll find a glossary of terms to translate insurance jargon, a decision-making worksheet you can actually use, and sample scenarios pulled from real client stories. These aren't fluff — they're practical, proven tools I use every day with real people who've stood exactly where you're standing now. My goal is for you to finish this book with more than just clarity — I want you to walk away with resources you can lean on when the next decision comes up.

One quick note before we begin: You'll see a few examples throughout this book based on New Jersey plans. That's where I live and work — and where many of my clients are located — so it's the lens I know best. But Medicare is a federal program. The structure of how these plans work is the same no matter where you live. You may just need to check the specifics in your area to see what carriers are available.

Thank you again for choosing this book. I hope it gives you peace of mind, clarity, and the confidence to move forward in your Medicare journey — on your terms.

📖 chapter 1: welcome to what comes next

If you're holding this book, chances are you've already enrolled in Medicare Parts A and B — and now you're staring at a fork in the road that nobody told you was coming.

You followed the rules. You got your red, white, and blue Medicare card. You might've even breathed a sigh of relief when it came in the mail, thinking, *"Great. That's handled."* But then, all of a sudden, you started hearing about other plans, new deadlines, and things like Part D, Advantage, Medigap, enrollment windows, prior authorizations, drug tiers, and more. It doesn't take long before you realize: **just having A and B doesn't mean you're done. It means you're just getting started.**

That's where most people begin to feel stuck.

At this point in your Medicare journey, you're faced with three main paths forward:

- ☑️ Stick with Original Medicare and add a Medigap (Supplement) plan along with a standalone Part D prescription drug plan.
- ☑️ Choose a Medicare Advantage plan (Part C), which bundles most benefits under one private carrier.
- ☑️ Keep your employer or retiree coverage, if you're fortunate enough to have it.

That third option — employer or union retiree coverage — sounds simple on the surface. But the truth is, many people don't have access to it at all. Some employers don't offer anything for retirement. Others might offer a retiree plan that seems generous but comes with limitations that only become obvious once you try to use it — like restricted provider access, limited drug coverage, or coordination issues with Medicare itself.

There's also a fourth path that applies to a specific group — veterans, military retirees, and their spouses. If you qualify for care through the VA, TRICARE, or CHAMPVA, your Medicare decisions may look a little different. These systems can work in tandem with Medicare — and in some cases, replace parts of it. We'll cover those in detail in Chapter 5. But for now, just know that if you're part of that military-connected group, your situation has its own set of rules and timing traps that are worth understanding fully.

It's not uncommon for clients to tell me, *"I thought I had good retiree coverage, but now I'm paying more than my neighbor who just signed up on his own."* That doesn't mean employer plans are bad — it just means they're not always the best deal. And in many cases, they're structured to benefit the group as a whole, not tailored to individual needs.

In some situations, these plans act as **secondary coverage** — meaning they only pay after Medicare has covered its portion. In others, they might replace certain parts of Medicare entirely by offering a group Advantage plan or bundled pharmacy benefits. And while that may sound convenient, it can come with trade-offs: smaller provider networks, fewer options for customization, or plan rules that aren't obvious until you're in the middle of a medical situation.

You may also be balancing more than just your own needs. For example, if your spouse is under 65 and depends on your retiree coverage, switching to an individual Medicare plan could leave them without affordable insurance. That's not a minor concern — it's one of the most common reasons people stay on employer coverage longer than they'd like to.

It's also worth pointing out that retiree plans aren't always "free." Some come with monthly premiums, limited drug coverage, or hidden coordination gaps that create confusion at the pharmacy or billing office. And once you leave an employer plan, you may not be able to go back — or you may face higher costs if you try.

Even if this doesn't apply to you directly, it's still useful knowledge. You may have a spouse who's covered under your employer plan, or a friend weighing similar choices. Medicare conversations don't happen in a vacuum. What you understand today could help someone you care about tomorrow.

We'll explore how to evaluate retiree and employer coverage more fully in Chapter 4, including how to weigh it against individual market options like Medigap or Medicare Advantage. But it's worth planting the seed now: **just because you have employer coverage doesn't automatically mean it's your best or only option.**

That said, for most people reading this, the real decision will come down to just two choices:

- ✅ Stick with Original Medicare + Medigap + Part D
- ✅ Medicare Advantage Plan
- ✅ Employer or retiree coverage (if available)

And making the right choice here requires more than comparing premiums. It means understanding how each system operates — how care is accessed, how much financial risk you're taking on, and what kind of flexibility you want to protect down the line.

This is where most of the confusion begins. Because on paper, both options seem to promise "comprehensive" coverage. But the way they deliver that coverage is very different.

When clients come to me, they're often surprised to learn that Medicare isn't just "one card." That red, white, and blue card — the one from the government — gives you access to Medicare Parts A and B. That's hospital and outpatient coverage. It's your foundation. But by itself, it doesn't cover prescriptions. It doesn't include dental, vision, or hearing. And most importantly, it leaves you exposed to **20% coinsurance on almost every medical bill — with no annual cap.**

Let that sink in: Original Medicare doesn't have a maximum out-of-pocket limit. That means if you get sick and rack up $100,000 in medical bills, you could be responsible for $20,000 or more out of pocket. That's why almost nobody sticks with Original Medicare alone — it's just too risky.

To protect yourself, you need something that fills those gaps. That's where **Medigap** and **Medicare Advantage** come in. These two systems solve the same problem in completely different ways.

Think of it like choosing between two cars. Both will get you where you need to go. One has all the bells and whistles built into the dashboard — that's your Advantage plan. The other lets you install each feature separately — that's your Medigap with standalone Part D. But how you maintain them, how they respond in bad weather, how much they cost to fix, and how flexible they are on the road? That's where the real differences lie.

One isn't necessarily better than the other. But one is usually a better fit for **you.**

The problem is, most people don't get that kind of explanation. Instead, they get bombarded with ads that say things like "Get your benefits now!" or "You could be getting more from Medicare!" You see commercials with smiling seniors talking about money back in their Social Security checks, $0 premiums, free dental, and more. And while some of those benefits may be real, they're often attached to specific Advantage plans with specific trade-offs.

It's not that the plans are lying — it's that they're speaking a different language.

That's where I come in.

As a licensed broker, I've helped thousands of people navigate this exact point in their Medicare decision-making. And I can tell you from experience: the problem isn't that people don't want to learn — it's that the system doesn't make it easy to understand what matters.

So, let's start from the beginning — no hype, no pressure, no noise.

Just a simple breakdown of what your two main options are, how they work, and what you need to consider before choosing a path that could impact your care and finances for years to come.

Because unless someone gives you a clear map, it's hard to know what road you're even standing on — let alone where it leads.

medicare advantage: simpler on the surface, more structured in practice

Medicare Advantage (Part C) plans are offered by private insurance companies that contract with Medicare. When you join one, Medicare pays that company to administer your benefits. You no longer get your care directly through Original Medicare. Instead, the private company becomes your new gatekeeper — managing your care, coordinating your services, and handling your bills.

Most Medicare Advantage plans include **Part D prescription drug coverage**, along with other extras like dental, vision, hearing, and even gym memberships. These bundled benefits are often marketed as a major plus, and for some people, they really are.

In many counties, you can find Advantage plans with **$0 monthly premiums**, low primary care copays, and even transportation services or over-the-counter allowances. But there's a catch: these plans are built on networks. That means the doctors and hospitals you can use are limited to the

plan's approved list. If your doctor isn't on that list, you'll either pay more — or won't be able to see them at all unless it's an emergency.

Depending on your county and the carrier, some networks are wide and well-integrated. Others are narrow and frustrating. And not all doctors who accept Medicare take Advantage plans — a detail that surprises many people when it's already too late.

Another thing to keep in mind is **prior authorization**. While fewer plans today require referrals to see a specialist — especially in PPO options — most Advantage plans still use prior authorizations for certain services. This could include things like outpatient surgery, home health, or expensive imaging. It doesn't mean you won't get the care — but it means your doctor will have to request approval, and the insurance company has the right to deny or delay based on their criteria.

That said, many clients find Medicare Advantage fits them well — especially if they're healthy, don't travel much, and want everything in one place.

medigap + part d: higher premiums, more predictable protection

On the other side of the fork is **Medigap** — also called Medicare Supplement — paired with a standalone **Part D** plan.

In this setup, Original Medicare stays in place as your primary insurance. You go to any doctor or hospital in the country that accepts Medicare, with no need to check network directories. After Medicare pays its share, your Medigap plan picks up the rest — depending on the plan type you choose.

For most of my clients, the three most common Medigap options are **Plan G**, **Plan N**, and **Plan F**. Plan F is no longer available to people who became eligible for Medicare after January 1, 2020 — but those who already had it can keep it, and some are even grandfathered in from earlier years. Plan G and Plan N are the next most popular, and we'll break them down in detail later in the book.

The key advantage of Medigap is **freedom** — no networks, no referrals, and no guessing. You'll typically pay more each month, but you avoid most unexpected medical bills down the road. And for those who see multiple specialists or manage chronic conditions, that peace of mind can be priceless.

The trade-off? You'll need to shop separately for a Part D drug plan, which comes with its own deductible and formulary rules. You'll also pay monthly premiums for both the Medigap and the Part D plan. **Medigap premiums are based on your age, sex, and health history — not your zip code.** And while Part D premiums vary by plan, they're set by the carriers and have nothing to do with your individual characteristics. For many people, the stability and nationwide access to care that this setup provides is worth the extra monthly cost.

real talk: why people hesitate — and why that matters

I've seen it again and again: people freeze up when faced with this decision.

They don't want to make the wrong choice. They don't want to overpay. And they're tired of the noise. So, they either default to what their friend chose, or what the first agent told them, or — worse — they sign up for something based on a commercial that sounded friendly at 6 p.m. on a Tuesday.

I don't blame them. When you're dealing with something as important as healthcare in retirement, fear is a natural reaction. And when you're overwhelmed, it's easier to pick the path that seems simplest than to slow down and dig in.

But here's the thing: Medicare isn't one-size-fits-all. What works beautifully for your neighbor might be a terrible fit for you. What sounds affordable today might be limiting in a year. What looks generous on paper might be hard to use when life gets messy.

That's why I never tell clients which option to choose. I lay it out. I ask the right questions. And then I watch for the moment when something clicks — when they realize, *"This is what matters most to me."*

Because once that's clear, the rest starts to make sense.

why this decision is so hard — and so personal

Every year, especially around October, I see it happen: clients who were calm in June become overwhelmed by fall. Their mailboxes fill with plan brochures, Medicare TV ads flood every commercial break, and their phones start ringing with calls from people they don't know promising "extra benefits."

It's not just marketing — it's psychological. When we're faced with too many choices and too much pressure, we tend to shut down. And with Medicare, that shut-down can come at a cost.

One client told me, "I picked my plan based on the one that called me the most." Another said, "I didn't even know I had a choice. I thought everyone just picked the free one." It's not that they weren't smart — it's that the system didn't give them a clean, quiet space to understand what was actually happening.

This book is that space.

And here's the truth: while both Medicare Advantage and Medigap + Part D are valid choices, they function so differently that choosing between them **without understanding the structure is like picking a car based on the paint color.** It might look good in the driveway, but what happens when it snows? Or when you need to drive across the country? Or if the trunk doesn't fit your luggage?

That's why I never rush people into choosing. I want you to understand what you're choosing *between* — and how that choice might affect you now, next year, or five years from now.

real differences that matter (even if they don't show up on the brochure)

Let's take two people, both age 67, both healthy, both living in the same county. One chooses an Advantage plan with no premium, bundled drug coverage, and $0 primary care visits. The other chooses Medigap Plan G and a $15/month Part D plan. Both seem happy — at first.

But now imagine both need outpatient surgery. The Advantage member might pay 20% up to their plan's out-of-pocket max — maybe $1,000 or more depending on the plan. The Medigap member pays the Part B deductible — $240 in 2025 — and that's it. No coinsurance. No surprises.

Or say they both travel to visit family for the holidays. The Medigap member can see any provider nationwide who accepts Medicare. The Advantage member needs to check if their plan has out-of-area coverage — and if not, they're limited to emergency care.

These aren't minor differences. They affect your **access to care**, your **financial risk**, and your **freedom to move around without worrying about paperwork or approval forms.**

But again — some people *don't* travel. Some *do* want an all-in-one plan. And for many people with tight budgets, that $0 premium on an Advantage plan feels like a gift. The point isn't to say one is better — it's to understand what each path actually offers, so your decision isn't made by accident.

what i see most often: clients who didn't know there were rules

One of the hardest conversations I have each year is with someone who says, *"I didn't realize I couldn't switch."* They thought Medicare was flexible — like changing phone providers — where you could move in and out of plans whenever you wanted. But Medicare doesn't work that way.

There are real limits on when and how you can switch — especially between Medigap and Medicare Advantage. Here's how I break it down for clients:

✅ If you start with **Medigap** during your Initial Enrollment Period (or if you qualify for **guaranteed insurability**), you're accepted — no health questions, no denials.

✅ But if you leave Medigap and try to come back later, you'll usually face **medical underwriting**. That

means filling out a health questionnaire — and yes, you can be denied or charged more based on your conditions.
✅ **One-time exception:** Many Medigap carriers offer a 12-month "test drive" period. If you're already in a Medigap plan and decide to try Medicare Advantage, you typically have one year to return to your original Medigap policy **without underwriting** — but only if you go back to the **same insurer, same plan letter, and same monthly premium.** Stay longer than a year, and that safety net disappears.

This part confuses a lot of people — especially because there's a separate protection called the **Medigap Trial Right**. It doesn't work differently from the 12-month "test drive" rule mentioned earlier — in fact, **it's the same concept**. I introduced it earlier in simpler terms to help make the idea easier to grasp before diving into the official name.

The **Medigap Trial Right** is a **federal protection**, not tied to any specific insurance company. It allows you to try a Medicare Advantage plan after enrolling in Medigap — and gives you the right to return to a Medigap plan **without medical underwriting**, as long as you do so within the allowed 12-month window. In simpler terms, it's the same "test drive" idea we discussed — but formally recognized by Medicare and subject to specific rules.

⭐ **To keep things simple going forward, I'll refer to this as the "Medigap Trial Right" throughout the rest of the book.**

Timing Isn't Just About Deadlines — It's About Leverage

One of the most important things I try to explain to clients is that **Medicare is about more than picking a plan.** It's about knowing when to act — and understanding that every delay or assumption can affect what options are available later.

People don't always feel the urgency, especially if they're healthy or still working. But just because you feel good today doesn't mean you'll feel the same next year — or that the rules won't shift in a way that closes a door you assumed would always be open.

In this system, **timing creates leverage** — and failing to act during the right window can quietly erase your ability to choose freely later on.

👤 Client B: Missed the Leverage Window

Client B had already enrolled in Medicare Parts A and B at age 65 but stayed on his employer plan because he was still working full time. At 67, he retired and wanted to transition to a Medigap plan.

Luckily, coming off his employer coverage gave him access to a **Special Enrollment Period** — triggered by the loss of group insurance. He was able to sign up for a Medigap plan without underwriting, even with a heart condition on his record.

But here's the twist: he hadn't planned ahead. He thought he'd have more time to compare options after retiring, but now he was racing the clock — reviewing premiums, Part D drug coverage, and Medicare Advantage plans all at once. It was overwhelming. The paperwork, the plan comparisons, the drug formularies — he nearly gave up and picked the first plan he saw.

He didn't — but I've seen many others who did. And not all of them got lucky.

The point here isn't just about getting Medigap without underwriting. It's about understanding how **certain windows give you power** — and if you wait too long, that power may disappear.

---

the psychology of medicare decisions

The truth is, Medicare is as much an emotional decision as a financial one. You're not just choosing a plan — you're choosing how you want to **engage with the healthcare system** for the foreseeable future.

✅ Do you want everything bundled together in one place?
✅ Do you prefer freedom and simplicity, even if it costs more upfront?
✅ Are you okay managing multiple cards, premiums, and drug formularies — or do you want one ID card and a single point of contact?

These are personal preferences, not right-or-wrong answers.

But what makes them tricky is that most people don't realize they're facing those questions at all. They think they're just signing up for "Medicare," when in reality, they're building a structure around their care, their finances, and their peace of mind.

The consequences of that decision don't always show up right away. Sometimes it takes six months. Sometimes it takes a diagnosis. Sometimes it's just one bad billing experience that makes someone say, "I had no idea it worked like this."

why this book exists — and what comes next

When I first helped my mom through Medicare, I didn't know any of this either. I was learning while she was living it. That's what made me so committed to mastering the system. I saw how easily smart, caring people could get misled, confused, or caught in coverage they didn't fully understand.

Over the years, I've helped thousands of clients — each one different, each one with a unique combination of health needs, financial goals, family support, and risk tolerance. Some knew what they wanted. Most didn't. But every single one of them needed **a clean, honest breakdown** of what their options were and how those options played out over time.

That's what this book is here to give you.

No fluff. No sales pitch. No pressure. Just a clear path through a very murky system — one you shouldn't have to decode on your own.

if you're still feeling unsure — that's normal

You don't have to know everything right now. You don't need to become an expert. But you do need to understand the structure you're choosing — and how that structure affects your freedom, your financial risk, and your ability to respond when life throws you a curveball.

As you keep reading, we're going to walk through each major path — Medicare Advantage, Medigap, Part D, and employer coverage — with real examples, tools, and clarity you won't find in a government booklet or a TV ad.

I'll show you what these plans actually look like. I'll explain what to ask, what to watch for, and how to avoid common traps that cost people thousands of dollars or delay care when they need it most.

And at the end of it all, I hope you'll walk away feeling one thing above all else: **confident.**

Confident that you understand the system. Confident that you know what questions to ask. And confident that no matter which path you choose, it was a decision **you** made — clearly, intentionally, and with eyes wide open.

chapter 2: medicare advantage – what you need to know

medicare advantage: what you're really signing up for

At first glance, Medicare Advantage plans seem like a simple solution. Everything is bundled: hospital coverage, medical services, drug coverage, and even extras like dental or vision. All of it comes under one card — and often, with a $0 monthly premium. That sounds great. But when you look closer at how these plans actually work, the story becomes more layered.

For some people, Medicare Advantage offers real value. For others, it creates frustration they didn't expect — especially when it comes to access, flexibility, and out-of-pocket costs. What matters most is understanding how the system is built before you join it.

drug coverage is included — but it comes with limits

Most Medicare Advantage plans include a built-in Part D prescription drug plan. This means you don't have to search for or manage a separate drug plan like you would if you chose Medigap. It's an all-in-one design that works well for people who want fewer moving parts.

But here's where the trade-offs begin:

> ✅ You can't change your drug plan without changing your entire Advantage plan. If your medications change mid-year and your plan doesn't cover them well — or at all — you'll need to wait for the next opportunity to switch. That may happen during the **Annual Enrollment Period (AEP)** from October 15 to December 7, the **Open Enrollment Period (OEP)** from January 1 to March 31, or a **Special Election Period (SEP)** if you qualify due to a life event or change in status.
> ✅ Each plan has its own drug formulary — the list of medications it covers. Some plans offer great coverage on generics but place significant restrictions or higher costs on name-brand medications.
> ✅ You may encounter rules like **step therapy** or **prior authorization.** These policies can delay access or force you to try lower-cost medications before your prescribed drug is approved, even when your doctor already knows what works best for you.

If your medication needs are minimal and stable, these limitations may not affect you much. But for people managing multiple prescriptions or complex conditions, the lack of flexibility can become a major frustration — especially when timing matters and options feel limited.

dental, vision, and hearing: what you're really getting

Advantage plans are heavily marketed for their "extra benefits" — especially dental, vision, and hearing. And yes, those benefits are included in many plans. But they're not always what people expect.

> ✅ **Dental** coverage often includes two cleanings and a basic exam per year. Major work like crowns, implants, or bridges may only be partially covered — or capped at a few hundred dollars annually.
> ✅ **Vision** benefits typically include a routine eye exam and a small allowance for glasses or contacts. But coverage for medical vision issues (like cataract surgery) still falls under the medical side.
> ✅ **Hearing** coverage may include a basic test and a discount on hearing aids. But the actual cost-sharing and quality of coverage can vary by brand and provider.

Are these perks helpful? Absolutely. But they're best viewed as supplemental — not as replacements for full dental or vision insurance.

the growing appeal of otc allowances

One area where Advantage plans have genuinely improved in recent years is the **quarterly Over-the-Counter (OTC) allowance.** This benefit gives members a set dollar amount — often $25 to $100 per quarter — that can be used to purchase non-prescription health items.

Depending on the plan, this allowance may be delivered through a preloaded card for in-store use or through a catalog-style ordering system. Either way, it's a practical perk, especially for people managing chronic conditions or trying to stay ahead of small health issues at home.

While OTC allowances won't change your overall medical costs, they can help reduce your out-of-pocket spending on everyday items.

veterans and the giveback plans

If you're a veteran receiving care through the VA, you might wonder why you'd even consider enrolling in a Medicare Advantage plan. After all, the VA already covers a broad range of services — and you may not need to use another provider.

But in practice, many veterans do enroll in Advantage plans — often not for the care itself, but for the savings.

Certain Medicare Advantage carriers offer what's called a **Part B giveback plan** — a plan that reduces the amount you pay for your monthly Part B premium. In 2025, the standard Part B premium is $174.70. Giveback plans might cover part of that cost — or all of it — depending on the plan and where you live.

Why is this valuable?

- ✅ You're still required to pay the Part B premium — even if you receive care exclusively through the VA. Enrolling in a giveback plan helps reduce or eliminate that monthly cost.
- ✅ There's **no conflict** between VA benefits and Medicare Advantage. You can use either system — or both — depending on your needs. You might use VA for primary care and prescriptions, and your Advantage plan for dental, vision, or urgent care outside the VA system.
- ✅ Many veterans like the flexibility of having civilian coverage as a backup — especially if travel, access delays, or certain services aren't easily handled through VA facilities.

It's not about replacing one system with another. It's about creating **layers of coverage** that serve your unique needs — and possibly saving hundreds or even thousands of dollars per year in the process.

network access: the real trade-off

Here's where Medicare Advantage differs most from Original Medicare with Medigap: network structure.

Advantage plans are built around managed care networks. That means you must use doctors, hospitals, and providers that are in-network — or you may pay more, or in some cases, all of the bill.

✅ **HMO plans** require you to stay in-network for all non-emergency care. Out-of-network services typically aren't covered unless it's urgent or an emergency.
✅ **PPO plans** offer more flexibility. You can see out-of-network providers, but you'll pay more — and coverage might be limited depending on the service.

This model isn't inherently bad. In fact, it mirrors what many people had while working — an HMO or PPO through their employer. But it does mean you have to be more intentional about your providers.

what about referrals in 2025?

This is a question that comes up a lot — especially from people who remember when Advantage plans required constant referrals for everything.

As of 2025, **referrals are rarely required.** In most Advantage plans, especially in New Jersey and other major markets, members can go directly to in-network specialists without needing approval from their primary care doctor.

In rare cases — usually due to the provider's internal policy or for certain high-cost treatments — a referral might still be requested. But across the board, this barrier has largely disappeared.

That change alone has made Advantage plans more attractive to people who want direct access without jumping through hoops. Still, it's always smart to double-check when scheduling a new visit, just in case the provider's office has its own protocols.

What It All Means

So far, the Advantage system may sound appealing — bundled benefits, no referrals, drug coverage included, extra perks like OTC allowances, and possible savings for veterans.

But this is just the surface.

In the next section, we'll look beyond the marketing and dig into what it really costs to use an Advantage plan — the maximum out-of-pocket limits, how prior authorizations work, and how networks and plan rules affect real people when real health issues show up.

understanding the maximum out-of-pocket (moop)

One of the biggest misconceptions about Medicare Advantage is that if your plan has a $0 premium, you won't spend much out of pocket. But that's not how the system works. Medicare Advantage plans are designed around cost-sharing — and while they do include protections, the limits are often higher than most people expect.

Every Advantage plan is required to set an annual **maximum out-of-pocket limit**, known as the **MOOP**. This is the ceiling for how much you'd pay for **Part A and Part B–covered services** in a calendar year — hospital stays, outpatient procedures, doctor visits, diagnostic imaging, and so on. It does **not** include prescription drug costs.

In 2025, the **federal maximum** is **$8,850**, but that's just the legal cap. Many carriers set theirs lower — or higher, depending on plan type and network flexibility. Based on current plans in the New Jersey market, including UnitedHealthcare, here's what we're seeing:

✅ MOOPs can range anywhere from **$7,550 to $14,000**, depending on the plan, whether it's an HMO or PPO, and whether you're staying in-network or going out-of-network.
✅ Most HMO plans stay in the **$7,550–$8,550** range for in-network care. The **2025 AARP Medicare Advantage Patriot (HMO)** by UnitedHealthcare, for example, has a **$8,550 in-network MOOP** — a figure that reflects the higher end of what's considered common.
✅ PPO plans may advertise broader access, but they come with trade-offs. Many list **separate MOOPs** for in-network vs. out-of-network services, and the out-of-network MOOP can be **as high as $13,300–$14,000** depending on the carrier.

Here's what else you should know about how MOOP works:

- ✅ **The MOOP resets each calendar year.** If you hit your limit in October due to a major health event, it starts over again in January — and you begin a new climb toward the cap.
- ✅ **Prescription drugs are not counted** toward this total. Part D expenses (even if bundled with the plan) have their own cost structure, which we'll talk about in Chapter 3.
- ✅ **MOOP only protects you if care is authorized and in-network.** In PPOs, out-of-network services apply toward a separate out-of-network MOOP — often much higher.

Many people never hit the MOOP. But if you develop a chronic illness, need surgery, or experience complications, you can hit it in one unpredictable year — especially if your plan uses coinsurance (a percentage) rather than flat copays.

---

real example: when every day matters

A client I worked with — let's call him

👤 **Client C** — had been enrolled in a Medicare Advantage plan for three years with no issues. He was healthy, saw his primary care doctor once a year, and liked the extra perks like dental and the OTC benefit. It was simple and affordable — until it wasn't.

One October morning, he woke up with severe abdominal pain. His doctor suspected appendicitis and ordered a CT scan. But because his HMO plan required prior authorization for that type of imaging, the request had to be submitted to the insurance company.

It took four business days to get approval. By the time it came through, he had already gone to the ER. His appendix had ruptured. He ended up needing emergency surgery and spent **six days in the hospital** due to complications. The total charges — after insurance — triggered **nearly $5,500 in out-of-pocket expenses** within three months.

But here's the part most people miss:

His MOOP was **$8,550** — so even after the $5,500 in costs, he still had **$3,050 left** to potentially pay before the end of the calendar year. If any other serious issue had come up — more testing, rehab, outpatient surgery — he could've reached the full MOOP quickly.

And then on **January 1**, that protection resets. If he remained in the same plan (and if the carrier didn't increase the MOOP), he'd start back at **$0** and begin the process again.

Would this have happened with Medigap? Possibly — but differently. He wouldn't have needed pre-approval for the scan, and his **total out-of-pocket cost under Plan G in 2025 would have been just $240** — the annual Part B deductible. That's it.

Again, this isn't about saying one system is bad. It's about **understanding the structure** — because in Medicare

Advantage, timing and process can have real financial consequences.

Client D: PPO Flexibility — But at a Price

Client D chose a **PPO Advantage plan** because of the flexibility it offered. She lived in New Jersey but spent winters in Florida, and wanted the option to see doctors out of state without having to change plans or pay full cost.

During her stay in Florida, she scheduled a dermatology appointment for a suspicious spot on her arm. She checked to make sure the provider was in-network and confirmed a **40% coinsurance rate for out-of-network care** — a trade-off she was comfortable with.

The visit went smoothly, and the biopsy was performed on site. But a few weeks later, she received a **$700 bill** for lab testing — from a provider who wasn't part of the out-of-network coverage agreement. The dermatology clinic used an independent lab, which billed separately and wasn't covered under the PPO terms of her UnitedHealthcare plan.

She wasn't upset with the plan itself. In fact, she liked having the ability to receive care out of state — and she still saved money compared to paying 100% out-of-pocket. But she realized that "out-of-network" doesn't mean "fully covered," especially when services are split between multiple providers.

Lesson learned: In PPOs, **each provider must be verified individually** — even if they're under the same roof. Billing is often separate, and if one piece of the process falls outside your network, the cost can rise quickly.

---

so how do you choose wisely?

Now that we've peeled back the layers on how Medicare Advantage really works — the bundled benefits, the network structures, the prior authorizations, and the potential out-of-pocket exposure — the natural next question is: *How do you choose between Advantage and Medigap?*

The truth is, there's no one-size-fits-all answer. What works well for your neighbor may be a poor fit for you. What felt like a smart decision three years ago might be completely wrong today. The key is to look at your **personal health needs, lifestyle, and financial situation** through the right lens.

So, let's go beyond the marketing language and surface-level comparisons. Here's what I walk my clients through every day when helping them choose a plan:

Step 1: Understand How You Actually Use Healthcare

Start by answering honestly:

✅ How often do you visit your doctors?
✅ Do you have any specialists you see regularly?
✅ Are there treatments or procedures you expect to need in the next 12 months?
✅ How complex are your medications?

If you have frequent appointments, multiple chronic conditions, or use brand-name medications, the structure of Medicare Advantage — with its cost-sharing and pre-approvals — could become burdensome. In those cases, Medigap may provide **more predictable and flexible coverage**, even if the monthly cost is higher.

But if you're healthy, rarely see the doctor, and don't rely on ongoing medications, then a well-structured Advantage plan could be a smart way to save money and keep things simple — especially if you're comfortable navigating networks.

Even if you do take maintenance medications, as long as they're **commonly prescribed generics** — like lisinopril, carvedilol, atorvastatin, or metformin — an Advantage plan may still serve you well. Most plans cover these drugs at a low or no copay, particularly when filled through a preferred pharmacy.

Step 2: Map Out Your Doctor Access

This part is often overlooked. Don't just assume your doctor accepts a plan — **check it, and check it again.** Ask the provider's office directly. If you're working with a broker or licensed agent, they should be able to verify your primary care doctor, specialists, and preferred hospital systems across all available Advantage plans in your area.

Things to look out for:

☑ Is your provider *in-network*?
☑ Are they *still participating* in the plan you're considering for 2025?
☑ Do they have *hospital privileges* at the facilities you'd want to use?

One of the most frustrating experiences is signing up for a plan, scheduling a visit, and then learning — at the front desk — that your doctor doesn't accept it. This happens more than you'd think. Advantage networks change annually. So, a provider you saw this year may not be participating next year.

With Medigap, you don't have to worry about any of this. If the provider accepts Medicare, you're good to go — no network restrictions.

Step 3: Calculate the Real Costs — Not Just the Premium

One of the biggest traps people fall into is judging a plan based on its monthly premium alone. Yes, Medicare Advantage plans often have **$0 premiums** — but that doesn't mean you won't spend money.

Here's what I help clients tally when comparing:

Feature	Medicare Advantage	Medigap + Part D
Monthly premium	Usually $0 – $75	$150 – $300+
Primary care copays	$0 – $20	$0 – $20
Specialist copays	$10 – $50	$0 – $20
Hospital admission	$200 – $350/day (for 5–7 days)	$0
Outpatient surgery	20% coinsurance or fixed copay	$0
Diagnostic imaging	$100 – $300	$0
Part D cost	Included	$0 – $100 extra
Annual max out-of-pocket	$7,550 – $14,000	~$240 (Part B deductible only)

Even when you total the **monthly premiums**, **Part B deductible**, and the few small copays you might encounter under Medigap, the **overall annual cost is still usually far lower** than the MOOP for an Advantage plan — especially in a year where your health changes or unexpected needs arise.

That's the real comparison: not just what you pay when things go well — but what protection you have when they don't.

👤 Client E: Healthy, Low-Maintenance, and Budget-Conscious

Client E came to me at age 65, in excellent health and focused on minimizing his cost. No prescriptions. No recent hospitalizations. He played tennis three times a week and didn't want to "waste money" on something he might never use.

His top priority? Keeping costs low.

We reviewed a few **zero-premium Medicare Advantage plans** in his area. One stood out with **$0 primary care visits, $25 copays for specialists**, and a **$7,550 MOOP (maximum out-of-pocket).** The plan also included extra benefits like **dental, vision**, and a **$100-per-quarter Over-the-Counter (OTC) allowance** — which easily covered vitamins, cold medications, and some first-aid essentials.

He was impressed. "Why would anyone pay more when this gives me everything I need?" he asked — and it was a valid question.

At that point, we talked about the **"what ifs"** — not as a scare tactic, but simply to help him think ahead. What would happen if his health changed in a few years? What if he started seeing several specialists or traveled more? We also discussed how Advantage plans handle that: while he'd still be covered, he'd likely have to navigate **copays, coinsurance**, and possibly **prior authorizations** depending on the service.

We looked at Medigap Plan N as a comparison. It had higher monthly premiums and required purchasing a standalone Part D plan, but came with predictable costs and no network restrictions. Ultimately, **both options fit his needs.** But after weighing them side by side, he chose to begin with Medigap — mostly for the simplicity and flexibility. "If I stay healthy, I can always reassess down the line," he said.

Three years later, he's still on Medigap — and still playing tennis. But what mattered wasn't just the plan he picked. It was that he made the decision **knowing how both paths work** — and how they adapt (or don't) when life changes.

👤 Client F: Busy Caregiver, Little Time for Complexity

Client F was in good health, but her life was anything but simple. She was a full-time caregiver for her husband and didn't want a plan that involved referrals, paperwork, or complicated billing. Her main request was straightforward: "I just need to know what's covered and what it's going to cost."

We sat down and reviewed both options.

On the **Medicare Advantage side**, she was eligible for a plan with **$0 primary care copays, $35 specialist visits**, and **extra benefits** like dental, vision, and transportation. It also included her current generic prescriptions at low or no cost — meds like lisinopril and metformin — and she appreciated that the plan bundled everything into one ID card.

Then we looked at **Medigap Plan G.** It came with a higher monthly premium and required a separate Part D plan, but gave her complete flexibility with **no network restrictions**, **no referrals**, and **minimal out-of-pocket costs** beyond the $240 annual Part B deductible.

In her case, **either option would have worked.** She wasn't managing complex health needs, and both plans covered her doctors. But after comparing side-by-side — and thinking about the mental bandwidth it would take to track authorizations or changing networks — she chose Medigap. "I already manage my husband's care," she told me. "I need mine to be simple."

She wasn't choosing because she thought one system was better overall — she just wanted to **remove complexity from her own plate**. And for her, that was worth the extra premium.

---

it's not just about health — it's about preference

Many people assume this decision is only about health status. But that's just one piece of the puzzle.

✅ Some healthy people still prefer Medigap — because they don't like surprises.
✅ Some people with chronic conditions choose Advantage — because they qualify for Special Needs Plans (SNPs) or don't mind using networks.
✅ Some veterans use Advantage giveback plans to offset their Part B premiums — while continuing to get care through the VA.
✅ Some people are fine navigating copays and referrals if it means they don't pay a premium each month.

What matters most is how you think about risk, convenience, and how involved you want to be in managing your coverage.

Choosing Isn't Forever — But Some Doors Close

One of the biggest myths in Medicare is the idea that "you can always change later." That's **partially true**, but not always in the direction people assume.

✅ You can switch Advantage plans every year during the **Annual Enrollment Period (AEP)** — October 15 to December 7.
✅ You can make one switch during the **Open Enrollment Period (OEP)** — January 1 to March 31.
✅ You may qualify for a **Special Election Period (SEP)** if your circumstances change — like moving, losing employer coverage, or qualifying for Medicaid or Extra Help.

But here's what doesn't come with guarantees:

Moving *into* a Medigap plan later in life.

If you didn't enroll in Medigap during your Initial Enrollment Period (IEP) or you're not eligible for guaranteed insurability, you'll likely have to pass **medical underwriting** to join a plan. That means answering health questions, and the carrier has the right to say no — or raise your premiums significantly.

That's why the **first decision matters so much.** It's not that you can't ever change. It's that **some options aren't guaranteed to be there** when you want them back.

The Psychology of the Decision

Let's talk about something rarely discussed in Medicare circles: **how people feel** about this decision.

Some clients want **control and predictability.** They like knowing, month to month, what they'll spend — even if it means paying more upfront. For them, Medigap + Part D feels safer and more transparent.

Others value **simplicity and bundling.** They're tired of being nickel-and-dimed by separate premiums and appreciate the streamlined experience of a well-structured Advantage plan. For them, it's about keeping everything in one place — even if that means navigating a few more plan rules.

Then there are those who feel anxious either way. They're not sure how to compare plans. They don't want to make a mistake. Some are afraid to ask questions because they think they'll sound "dumb." Others have gotten so many conflicting answers that they've stopped asking altogether.

That last group — the ones who feel lost in the noise — that's who this book is really for.

Not the people who already know everything.

Not the agents with every plan in their back pocket.

But for readers who simply want someone to **explain it clearly**, without pressure or jargon. Someone who sees the human side of the Medicare decision.

And if that's you, let me say it again:

You're in the right place.

the medicare decision tool: which path fits you best?

You can use this tool on your own or as a conversation guide with a trusted advisor. The more honest your answers, the more useful your direction will be. There's no grading scale here — just clarity.

1. How much do you travel or live away from your primary residence each year?

- ☐ I stay local year-round
- ☐ I travel seasonally (e.g., snowbird lifestyle)
- ☐ I split time between two states

If you travel or split residency, Medigap may offer greater flexibility with nationwide provider access. However, some Advantage carriers do offer limited or comparable out-of-state benefits — it's worth comparing both sides.

2. How many doctors or specialists do you currently see?

- ☐ Just a primary care doctor
- ☐ 1–2 specialists
- ☐ 3+ specialists or complex care coordination

If your provider list is long — or includes out-of-network specialists — Medigap may be a better fit. Still, don't overlook Advantage entirely; well-structured plans can accommodate multiple providers if networks are strong in your area.

3. What matters more to you: a low monthly premium or predictable costs during care?

- ☐ I want to minimize monthly premiums
- ☐ I'm okay paying more each month to avoid big surprises later

Advantage plans typically offer lower or $0 premiums but come with copays, coinsurance, and an annual max out-of-pocket (MOOP). Medigap plans cost more upfront, but limit your out-of-pocket exposure — especially if health issues arise.

4. Are your current doctors in-network with the Advantage plan you're considering?

- ☐ Yes, I've confirmed it
- ☐ No, I haven't checked yet
- ☐ I want full freedom of choice

Medigap lets you see any provider nationwide who accepts Medicare. Advantage networks vary and must be verified carefully. The person helping you should be able to confirm your primary care and specialists across all Advantage plans they represent.

5. How involved do you want to be in managing your coverage and care decisions?

- ☐ I prefer a plan that simplifies everything in one place, even if it has more structure
- ☐ I'm comfortable managing separate plans if it means more flexibility and fewer restrictions

Medicare Advantage plans bundle medical and drug coverage, and often include extras like dental and vision — but they may come with plan rules and provider limitations. Medigap + Part D requires managing two separate plans, but gives you more freedom and fewer access barriers.

6. Do you have employer or union retiree coverage?

- ☐ Yes
- ☐ No

If yes, you'll need to weigh how that coverage compares to what's available on the individual market — and how it affects your spouse or dependents if they're on your plan. We'll go deeper on this in Chapter 4.

7. How many medications are you currently taking?

- ☐ 0–2
- ☐ 3–5
- ☐ 6–7
- ☐ 8 or more

If you're only taking a few generics — like lisinopril, metformin, or atorvastatin — you'll likely find affordable options in both Medigap + Part D and Medicare Advantage.

But if you take multiple prescriptions, especially brand-name or tiered medications, it becomes even more important to check the **carrier's specific formulary** — not just the plan type.

Important note:

Stand-alone Part D plans (used with Medigap) and Advantage plans (which bundle drug coverage) **often use the same pharmacy benefit manager — especially within the same company.** For example, Aetna's stand-alone drug plan and its Advantage plan may share the same drug list. What differs is how each specific plan is structured.

Some Advantage plans that offer **richer ancillary benefits** (like dental, vision, or gym memberships) may offer **less generous drug coverage** — or include higher tiers and cost-sharing for the same medications.

That's why it's essential to **run your actual prescriptions through the plan's drug lookup tool** — whether it's a Part D plan or Advantage plan — before making a final choice.

Mark Your Review Dates Early

There are several key windows where you can review or change your Medicare plan. Knowing these ahead of time keeps you in control — and gives you the flexibility to act when needed.

✅ **Annual Enrollment Period (AEP): October 15 – December 7**
→ *Switch between Advantage plans, or between Advantage and Original Medicare with Part D.*
✅ **Open Enrollment Period (OEP): January 1 – March 31**
→ *Make a one-time change if you're already in a Medicare Advantage plan.*
✅ **Special Election Periods (SEP): April 1 – September 30**
→ *Available to certain individuals quarterly — including those with LIS (Extra Help), Medicaid, or qualifying life events.*
✅ **Medigap Trial Right (if applicable):**
→ *Within 12 months of first enrolling in Medicare Advantage after starting with Medigap.*

Set calendar reminders at your **6-month** and **11-month** marks if you're trying a plan for the first time. That gives you a chance to assess whether it's truly working — before key protections expire.

this isn't a lifetime lock-in

Medicare decisions feel big — and they are. But remember: this isn't a lifetime contract. While some doors (like guaranteed Medigap access) may close, **you'll always have opportunities to reassess.** Each year, review your providers, your prescriptions, and your plan benefits. What was right last year might not be right next year.

✅ Be proactive.
✅ Ask for help when needed.
✅ And always revisit your options when your life — or your health — changes.

where we're headed next

Now that you've seen what Medicare Advantage really looks like, it's time to explore the other side of the decision: **Medigap + Part D.**

In the next chapter, we'll walk through how Medigap works, what changes you need to know in 2025, and why — despite the higher monthly cost — it continues to be the go-to choice for many who want maximum control, simplicity, and long-term stability.

📘 chapter 3: medigap + part d – the freedom model

understanding medigap + part d: flexibility, control, and what it really costs

If Medicare Advantage is like an all-in-one package, then Medigap plus Part D is more of a custom build. It's not better or worse — it's just different. And for many people, especially those who want **maximum freedom and predictability**, this path provides peace of mind that's hard to replicate.

Let's break down what this combination actually looks like in 2025 — and how to know whether it fits your life now or in the future.

How It Works

Here's the basic structure:

☑️ **Original Medicare (Parts A & B):** Your foundation — you must have both active.
☑️ **Medigap (also called Medicare Supplement):** Helps cover the "gaps" in A & B, including coinsurance and deductibles.
☑️ **Part D (prescription drug coverage):** You buy this separately to cover medications.

This approach keeps your medical and drug coverage separate. That may sound like more to manage, but it gives you greater flexibility — especially when it comes to choosing providers and managing out-of-pocket costs.

why people choose medigap + part d

Most clients who choose this path are drawn to:

☑️ **Freedom to choose doctors nationwide** (as long as they accept Medicare)
☑️ **Fewer restrictions** — no networks, no referrals
☑️ **Predictable costs** — especially if you use healthcare often
☑️ **Lower risk during high medical years** (like after a surgery or new diagnosis)

You don't need permission to see a specialist. You won't face prior authorization barriers. And you'll never have to wonder if your out-of-state provider is "in-network." If they take Medicare, you're good.

2025 Medigap Plan Options: F, G, and N

In today's market, three Medigap plans dominate the conversation: **Plan G, Plan N, and Plan F.**

Let's start with a quick comparison:

Plan	Part B Deductible	Specialist Copays	Excess Charges	Eligibility
Plan F	$0	$0	Covered	Must have been eligible for Medicare before Jan 1, 2020
Plan G	$240 in 2025	$0	Covered	Open to all
Plan N	$240 in 2025	$20	Not covered	Open to all

- ✅ **Plan F** covers everything, including the Part B deductible — but it's only available to those who were Medicare-eligible before **January 1, 2020**. If you're new to Medicare now, you won't see Plan F on the menu.
- ✅ **Plan G** is the most comprehensive plan available to new enrollees in 2025. The only out-of-pocket cost on covered services is the **$240 Part B deductible**, which resets each calendar year. After that's met, Plan G picks up the rest.
- ✅ **Plan N** offers slightly lower premiums than Plan G, but with a few trade-offs. You'll pay $20 for some office visits, up to $50 for ER visits (waived if admitted), and you're responsible for any Part B excess charges, though these are rare in most states. Many clients see Plan N as a good value if they're in good health, barely see doctors, and want to save on premiums — as

long as they're comfortable with occasional copays.

Important reminder: Medigap premiums are based on your **age**, **gender**, and **health status** — **not your ZIP code.** This is different from Medicare Advantage plans, which are regionally priced and approved.

what about prescription drugs?

If you choose Medigap, you'll need to buy a **standalone Part D drug plan.** These are offered by private insurance companies and work independently of your Medigap policy.

☑ In 2025, the federal government introduced major reforms to make drug costs more manageable — most notably, the implementation of a **$2,000 annual cap on out-of-pocket drug costs.**
That means:
☑ Once you hit $2,000 in spending for the year, you won't pay anything more for covered drugs.
☑ This applies to **all** Part D plans — both standalone and those bundled inside Advantage plans.
☑ There's **no longer a catastrophic 5% phase** like in prior years. That phase has been eliminated entirely.

To appreciate how big this change is, here's a look at how **Part D worked in 2024:**

✅ **Deductible phase:** You paid 100% of your drug costs until you met your plan's deductible (up to $545).
✅ **Initial coverage:** After the deductible, you paid set copays or coinsurance until your total drug costs hit $5,030.
✅ **Coverage gap (donut hole):** You then paid 25% of the cost of brand-name and generic drugs.
✅ **Catastrophic stage:** After reaching $7,400 in true out-of-pocket costs, you entered catastrophic coverage — where you paid 5% of drug costs for the rest of the year.

Even though 5% may not sound like much, it added up fast — especially for expensive specialty drugs. And it **never stopped** until the calendar year ended.

Now in 2025, all of that complexity is gone. There's no donut hole. No catastrophic 5%. Just a $2,000 cap — and once you hit it, you're done.

This change brings much-needed simplicity and relief, especially for people who rely on high-cost medications. But it doesn't eliminate the need to carefully check **which drugs are covered by which plan** — because formularies still vary widely by carrier.

So, while some clients assume Medigap + Part D gives you "better" drug coverage, the truth is that **drug coverage**

quality depends on the carrier's formulary. The type of plan **only** becomes a factor within **Medicare Advantage** — where richer benefits in one area may mean trade-offs elsewhere, including the drug list.

Tip: Whether you choose Medigap + Part D or Medicare Advantage, always run your prescriptions through the plan's drug finder tool before enrolling. Each plan has its own **formulary, copays, and pharmacy network** — and those can affect your costs far more than the plan label itself.

real costs, real clients — how medigap plays out in the real world

Understanding coverage is one thing. Seeing how it applies in real life is something else entirely.

That's why I always bring real examples to the table — actual client scenarios (with details changed to protect privacy) to help make these decisions feel more grounded. Let's take a look at what this path really looks like for people just like you.

Client A: The Frequent Flier With Chronic Conditions

Client A was 70 when he came to me. A retired small business owner living in northern New Jersey, he had been diagnosed with COPD, high blood pressure, and diabetes. He saw four specialists regularly and had prescriptions that included both generics and a Tier 3 brand-name inhaler.

He didn't want surprises. His biggest fear was winding up in the hospital and getting a bill for thousands he didn't expect.

Here's what we put together:

✅ Medigap Plan G — $172/month
✅ Part D plan — $24/month
✅ Part B deductible (2025) — $240/year
✅ Monthly prescription cost after formulary check — about $64/month total
✅ No copays for doctor or specialist visits
✅ No referrals, no network worries

For him, the predictability mattered more than the premium. We tallied his monthly and annual projected spend:

Category	Monthly Cost	Estimated Annual Cost
Medigap Plan G Premium	$172	$2,064
Part D Premium	$24	$288
Part B Deductible	N/A	$240
Drug Copays	~$64	~$768
Total		**$3,360**

He reviewed the math, thought about his 5+ appointments a month, and said, "This isn't just insurance. This is peace of mind."

And he meant it.

👤 Client B: Early 70s, Moved From Another State

Client B relocated to New Jersey to be closer to her grandchildren. She had been on a Medigap Plan F from her previous state, paying $225/month — a premium that had increased steadily over the past few years. Because Plan F is no longer offered to newly eligible enrollees, it's become more expensive for those grandfathered in.

We reviewed her existing coverage and realized she could switch to Plan G — with nearly the same benefits, just minus the Part B deductible. Her new premium dropped to $165/month. A low-cost Part D plan fit her generics (all Tier 1) at $10/month. Her prescriptions cost about $8/month in copays.

Even with the $240 deductible on Plan G, she was still saving hundreds a year. The switch made sense — not just for her wallet, but for her peace of mind as well.

She told me, "I'd rather overpay a little than worry if something's covered." But after seeing the numbers, she realized she wasn't overpaying at all — she was just locking in consistency.

common medigap pricing in new jersey (2025 snapshot)

To give you a quick picture of what you might expect in the Garden State:

Plan Type	Age 65	Age 70	Age 75
Plan G	~$160–$180/month	~$175–$195/month	~$200–$225/month
Plan N	~$125–$140/month	~$140–$155/month	~$160–$175/month
Plan F*	~$190–$215/month	~$210–$235/month	~$235–$260/month

⭐ *These are estimates based on current rates from major carriers in New Jersey. Rates vary by age, sex, health history, and the specific insurance company. Your final price may be slightly different.*

And remember: these plans are standardized. A Plan G is a Plan G, no matter which company you choose — the only difference is the company and premiums.

switching medigap carriers? here's what to know

Some clients ask me, "Can I switch Medigap companies later if I find a better rate?"

The answer is yes — but not always without underwriting.

If you're healthy and pass medical questions, most carriers will let you switch. But if you've had recent health changes, it may be harder to qualify for a new plan — even if you're already on Medigap.

Important: If you're considering a switch, do it sooner rather than later. Waiting until health declines can lock you into your current rate — even if other companies lower theirs over time.

---

but what about advantage plan comparisons?

We'll get to those in the next chapter — with real cost and risk breakdowns using New Jersey plans like Clover and UnitedHealthcare.

For now, just know this: Medigap + Part D is not a second-tier option. It's not outdated or overly expensive. In fact, for people with specific needs — complex care, multiple specialists, frequent travel, or a desire for stability — it can be the most protective option available.

What it isn't, though, is simple. You need to put the pieces together. But once you do, it works incredibly well — and remains one of the most stable models in the entire Medicare system.

don't miss your window: enrollment timing and guaranteed issue

One of the biggest mistakes people make with Medigap is assuming they can enroll at any time without restrictions. But unlike Medicare Advantage — which allows plan changes every year during annual enrollment, open enrollment, and special election periods — Medigap doesn't work that way.

When you first become eligible for Medicare — meaning both Part A and Part B — you enter a seven-month window known as your **Initial Enrollment Period (IEP).** This includes the three months before your 65th birthday month, your birthday month, and the three months after. If both Part A and Part B become active during this window, you're granted what's called **guaranteed issue** — meaning you can enroll in any Medigap plan available in your area with **no medical questions**, regardless of your current health status.

If you miss this window, future enrollment into Medigap may require:

✅ Medical underwriting
✅ A detailed health questionnaire
✅ Possible denials based on pre-existing conditions
✅ Premium increases if you're accepted with risk factors

That's not meant to scare you — it's just the reality of how private Medigap insurers operate. They aren't required to accept you after that initial IEP unless you qualify for certain special election periods, like a **Medigap Trial Right** (explained in Chapter 2), or a **Special Enrollment Period (SEP)** triggered by **loss of employer coverage.**

⭐ **Pro Tip:** If you're healthy now and want the option of Medigap later, it's often best to lock it in when you're first eligible. If you delay and your health changes, your options may be limited.

what if you're still working at 65?

Many people delay Medicare enrollment because they're still working — and that's perfectly fine all employer insurance is considered creditable coverage.

Let's say you turn 65 but continue working and delay Part B until age 68. When you retire and activate Part B, you'll qualify for an SEP due to **loss of employer coverage**. And under federal law, this **does** trigger a new guaranteed issue period for Medigap — not at the insurer's discretion. It's an **eight-month window** starting from the date you lose your employer's coverage.

If you wait **too long** after your employer coverage ends — say, eight months or more — you could lose both your SEP and your guaranteed issue protections. In that case, you'd likely face

late enrollment penalties for Part B and **medical underwriting** when applying for Medigap. Medicare Advantage, on the other hand, can still be accessed via SEP without medical questions.

Late enrollment penalties apply only for **Part B** — and they're based on how long you waited after employer coverage ended. These penalties have **nothing to do with Medigap or Medicare Advantage**, and again, the SEP window is **eight months.**

And yes — your employer coverage is creditable, you won't face any late enrollment penalties **as long as you transition within the eight-month window** that begins when your employer coverage ends. This applies to both **Part B and Part D.** The only time penalties kick in is if you delay enrollment beyond that window — either for Medicare itself or for a Medigap plan that requires a standalone drug plan.

Switching from Advantage to Medigap: Not Always Easy

This is one of the most misunderstood parts of Medicare planning.

Some people think they can try Advantage for a few years and then "upgrade" to Medigap when they need more coverage. That's not always how it works.

If you start with Advantage and later decide to switch to Medigap:

✅ You must apply through a Medigap carrier
✅ You will be subject to medical underwriting
✅ Your application can be denied — especially if you've developed new health issues

There is **no trial right** for switching from Advantage to Medigap. Trial rights only apply when someone starts with Medigap, switches to Advantage, and then decides to return within a limited window. If you're moving the other direction — from Advantage to Medigap — underwriting is required, and acceptance is not guaranteed.

Don't Forget: If you're healthy, some carriers will still accept you outside of guaranteed issue. But if you've had a recent diagnosis, hospitalization, or surgery, many will decline your application — or offer a higher premium. That's why your **first choice matters.**

what makes medigap + part d different (and for whom)

It's not just about coverage levels — it's about lifestyle, predictability, and how you interact with the healthcare system.

This combination appeals to a certain mindset: people who want freedom, control, and simplicity in how they access care.

✅ See multiple specialists or anticipate complex care
✅ Travel frequently or live in multiple states
✅ Want to avoid referrals or authorization delays
✅ Prefer predictable costs — monthly **and** yearly — with **zero** surprises

It's not always the cheaper option up front. But it offers cost certainty and national flexibility, which can be invaluable for people managing ongoing care or who don't want to stress about networks and plan rules.

That doesn't mean it's right for everyone — especially if you're healthy and rarely use your insurance. But it's important to understand that this model isn't just "the expensive one." It's the **low-variability option** — and for many, that's worth the premium.

choosing the right medigap plan: what's actually different?

Once clients understand how Medigap works, the next question I almost always hear is:

"What's the difference between Plan G, Plan N, and the rest of the alphabet soup?"

Here's the good news: not all Medigap plans are created equal — but you don't need to learn every letter to make a smart decision. In fact, 90% of my Medigap-seeking clients end up choosing between just two options: **Plan G** or **Plan N.** The remaining 10% are clients who still have **Plan F** that may or may not look at Plan G or Plan N only because of the high monthly premiums.

Let's unpack what makes these two the most popular — and how to choose wisely.

Plan G – Maximum Simplicity, Highest Coverage

✅ $0 copays for doctor visits, hospital stays, surgeries, labs, and most outpatient care
✅ Covers all Medicare-approved charges after you meet the $240 Part B deductible
✅ No network restrictions — freedom to see any provider nationwide who accepts Medicare
✅ Premiums tend to be higher, but so is the peace of mind

That $240 deductible is a **one-time** deductible for 2025 and is subject to change annually. Premiums tend to be higher than Plan N because of no copays for doctor visits.

Plan N – Budget-Friendly with a Few Trade-Offs

✅ You'll pay up to $20 for doctor visits and up to $50 for emergency room visits (if not admitted)
✅ Doesn't cover Part B excess charges — rare, but possible if a provider doesn't accept Medicare's standard rates
✅ Still no networks or referrals
✅ Monthly premiums are often $20–$50 lower than Plan G, depending on age, sex, and health conditions

Zip code does not play a part in how much the premiums are.

What's the Same?

✅ National access to providers — go anywhere Medicare is accepted
✅ Full coverage of hospital (Part A) costs
✅ No prior authorizations or network hoops
✅ Stable, predictable out-of-pocket costs — especially during high-use years

So how do you choose?

It depends on your **budget.**

If you want a plan where you don't have to think about copays or coverage — Plan G is your answer. If you're relatively healthy, don't mind the occasional $20–$50 fee, and want to save on premiums — Plan N might be a better fit.

⭐ **Don't Forget:** These are the **same benefits** no matter the carrier. A Plan G from Aetna is the same as a Plan G from Mutual of Omaha — the only difference is premium cost, customer service, and rate increase history.

Rate increases happen annually; some companies are slightly higher than others. But on average they range anywhere from 5% to 10%.

why cheaper isn't always better

Sometimes, a lower premium looks tempting — especially when you're comparing options side by side. But there are a few hidden factors to consider:

- ✅ **Rate Stability:** Some carriers lure people in with low premiums, then raise rates aggressively each year. Ask how long the company has offered Medigap in your state and whether they've had any sharp increases recently.
- ✅ **Household Discounts:** Some companies offer 5–12% discounts if you and a spouse enroll with the same carrier — even if one of you chooses a different plan letter.
- ✅ **Customer Service & Claims Handling:** It's not just about price. If something goes wrong, will you be stuck in phone tree limbo? Some Medigap carriers are better than others when it comes to resolving claims and getting answers quickly.

From experience

- ✅ UnitedHealthcare and Humana tend to be expensive. Customer service isn't terrible, but their underwriting process is very strict.
- ✅ Horizon (may go by a different name in your state; Blue Cross Blue Shield), Aetna, and Cigna offer very competitive pricing. Customer service is pretty good, and their underwriting isn't as strict compared to the first two.

What Happens if You Move?

With Medigap, your plan goes where you go.

If you move to another state — say, from New Jersey to Florida — your Medigap coverage follows you, as long as you keep paying the premium.

- ✅ You do **not** need to change plans or reapply
- ✅ You can see any doctor who accepts Medicare in your new state
- ✅ Your coverage works the same way, even across **ALL** states

Zip code does **not** play a part in premiums.

All Medigap providers have **national footprints**. Clients do not need to do anything if they move other than keep paying their premiums.

Medigap and Part D: Don't Forget the Drug Plan

Remember: Medigap only fills the gaps in Part A and B. It doesn't include drug coverage — that's where **Part D** comes in.

Many clients assume they don't need a Part D plan if they're not taking prescriptions. But skipping it can lead to penalties — and costly gaps if you need a medication unexpectedly.

✅ Part D plans are offered by private insurance companies
✅ You can shop and enroll through Medicare.gov or with a broker
✅ Plans vary in monthly premium, formulary, and pharmacy network
✅ The best plan for you depends on your current prescriptions and preferred pharmacy

Pro Tip: Even if you're only taking generics now, it's still **mandatory** to enroll in the lowest-cost plan available in your area to avoid future penalties and ensure you have coverage if your health changes.

what if you have a medicare advantage plan now?

Some clients don't start with Medigap — they enroll in Medicare Advantage first, thinking it's simpler or more cost-effective. And it might be — for a time.

But as your needs change, and you want to switch to Medigap, here's the key detail: **you don't always get to make that switch easily.**

If you're past your original **IEP phase** — and you didn't start with Medigap — you'll need to pass **medical underwriting** to qualify. That means:

✅ Answering detailed health questions
✅ Possibly being declined based on medical history
✅ Losing access to predictable out-of-pocket costs if you're denied

Don't Forget: There is no Annual Enrollment Period for Medigap. You can apply anytime — but you will be **subject to medical underwriting** unless you're within a guaranteed issue window (like coming off employer coverage or receiving Medicare Parts A and B for the first time). ***There are no trial rights from Medicare Advantage to Medigap. Trial rights only exist when going from Medigap to Medicare Advantage.***

how to choose a standalone part d plan (and avoid surprises)

Medigap doesn't include drug coverage — so if you go with this route, you'll need to pair it with a standalone Part D plan. While these plans are often overlooked, they play a major role in your total costs and daily experience. The goal isn't to just "have coverage" — it's to find a drug plan that works for your specific medications, at the lowest cost, and with the fewest restrictions.

Here's how to approach that decision wisely.

Start with a List of Your Medications

✅ Write down the exact name of each prescription you take.
✅ Note the dosage and how often you fill it.
✅ Identify your preferred pharmacy — some plans offer steep discounts for "preferred network" pharmacies, so where you shop matters.

Use Medicare's Plan Finder Tool

✅ Go to Medicare.gov and enter your prescriptions.
✅ The tool will calculate your expected monthly and annual drug costs based on each available Part D plan.
✅ But don't stop at cost — review the formulary tiers, prior authorization rules, and preferred pharmacy networks as well.

Check for Coverage Restrictions

✅ Some drugs may require prior authorization, meaning your doctor has to submit paperwork before it's approved.
✅ Others might have step therapy, where you're required to try a cheaper alternative first.

✅ These rules can delay treatment and frustrate even the most patient clients.

Don't Overpay for Brand Loyalty

✅ It's common for clients to say, "I've had XYZ plan for years — I'll just stick with it."
✅ But formularies and copays can change every year. The plan that worked in 2024 may not be the best in 2025.

⭐ **Pro Tip:** Run your medication list through the Plan Finder every October during the Annual Enrollment Period (AEP). Even a small change in your prescriptions or a plan's copay structure could mean hundreds of dollars saved or lost.

NJ-Based Example: Choosing Part D Wisely

Let's walk through a real scenario from one of my New Jersey clients — we'll call her **Client I.**

👤 **Client I: Diabetic, On Multiple Medications**

Client I was 67, recently retired, and had just signed up for Medigap Plan G. She took six prescriptions, including metformin, atorvastatin, and a newer drug for Type 2 diabetes.

During our review, we compared three popular Part D plans in her county. While all had similar premiums (around $20–

$25/month), the differences in her actual drug costs were huge:

Plan	Monthly Premium	Tier 3 Drug Copay	Preferred Pharmacy?	Estimated Annual Drug Cost
Plan A	$22	$47	Yes	$1,240
Plan B	$25	$35	No	$1,900
Plan C	$19	$42	Yes	$1,050

She almost chose Plan B — but it turned out her preferred pharmacy wasn't in-network, and her Tier 3 drug was priced higher as a result. By switching to Plan C and using a preferred pharmacy, she saved nearly $900 for the year — even though the monthly premium was slightly lower.

what about high-income penalties?

Here's something people don't always realize: if your income is above a certain level, you may have to pay extra for both Part B and Part D — and those surcharges apply no matter what type of Medicare plan you choose.

This is called **IRMAA** — Income-Related Monthly Adjustment Amount. It's based on your **tax return from two years ago.**

For 2025, IRMAA applies if your **individual income exceeds $103,000** or your **joint income exceeds $206,000** (based on 2023 tax data). Here's how that breaks down for Part D:

✅ You'll pay an extra $12.90 to $81/month *on top* of your Part D premium.
✅ The same income brackets apply to Part B, with even steeper surcharges.

Pro Tip: These charges are set by Medicare — not your plan. Even if you choose the cheapest drug plan available, IRMAA still applies if your income is above the limit. If your income has gone down due to retirement or life change, you can file Form SSA-44 to request a reduction.

---

medigap vs. advantage drug coverage: what's the real difference?

There's a common myth that Medicare Advantage plans have "better" drug coverage than standalone Part D. That's not quite true.

Both types of plans use a **formulary** — a list of covered drugs — and they both have tiers, copays, and cost-sharing rules. The key difference is this:

With Medicare Advantage:

- ✅ Your drug plan is bundled in.
- ✅ Formularies are specific to that Advantage plan.
- ✅ Some plans offer generous Tier 1 and Tier 2 pricing — but may limit choices on higher-tier drugs.
- ✅ Giveback or enhanced plans may offset premiums, but offer narrower drug coverage.

With Standalone Part D:

- ✅ You can shop plans independently based on your prescriptions.
- ✅ You aren't locked into one carrier's drug network.
- ✅ If your drug needs change, you can switch plans annually during AEP.

In both systems, the best outcomes happen when you match the plan to your medication profile — not the other way around.

real-world decision filters: which setup is right for you?

By now, you've seen that Medigap + Part D isn't one-size-fits-all — but it does tend to work best for certain client types.

- ✅ You take multiple medications and want freedom to shop drug plans annually.
- ✅ You want full control over which doctors and specialists you see.
- ✅ You anticipate needing complex or ongoing care and prefer no network restrictions.
- ✅ You prefer predictability, even if the premium is higher.
- ✅ You're a snowbird or planning to move in retirement and want seamless care in other states.

It's not always about "which is cheaper." It's about which path gives you the most confidence, clarity, and support for the way you actually use healthcare.

closing the chapter: medigap isn't just for the "sick" — it's for the prepared

There's a myth that Medigap is only for people who are sick or expect to have major health needs. That's not true.

✅ Many healthy clients choose Medigap because they value **predictability**, **doctor choice**, and **nationwide freedom.**
✅ Others choose it because they don't want to deal with red tape or changing networks.
✅ Some simply prefer to know that once they enroll, their plan won't change year after year — unlike many Advantage plans that adjust benefits annually.

As one client put it:

"I hope I never need to use my Medigap plan for anything major. But if something does happen, I don't want to worry about what's covered, or whether my specialist is in-network. I just want care."

That mindset — preparation, not fear — is what makes Medigap + Part D the right fit for many people.

And now that you've seen how it works, you can decide if that mindset feels right for you, too.

what to reflect on before you choose

Before we move on to the next chapter, take a moment to check in with yourself:

> ✅ Do you value nationwide access to providers over bundled extras?
> ✅ Are you someone who wants fixed, reliable medical costs — even if it means a higher monthly bill?
> ✅ Would you rather avoid annual changes, preapprovals, and worrying about coverage networks?
> ✅ Are you comfortable managing two separate plans (Medigap + Part D) for better long-term peace of mind?

If the answer is yes to most of these questions, Medigap + Part D may be a strong long-term fit.

But if your coverage is already provided through a **former employer or union** — or you expect to receive retiree benefits — you'll want to carefully evaluate how those benefits compare to individual Medigap and Advantage plans.

Because next, we're going to break down that third path: the one many people overlook until it's too late.

coming up next: employer & retiree plans

In Chapter 4, we'll shift our focus to **employer and union-sponsored retiree coverage** — what it looks like, how it coordinates with Medicare, and what to watch for before you make a decision.

> ✅ You'll learn how employer plans interact with Parts A and B.
> ✅ We'll cover what happens if you keep working past 65, or delay Part B enrollment.
> ✅ And we'll talk about how to compare your retiree plan to the individual market — including scenarios where keeping the employer plan makes sense, and situations where it doesn't.

Even if you don't have access to a retiree plan yourself, this chapter may help you advise a spouse, friend, or neighbor. Employer coverage is a part of the Medicare conversation — and understanding how it works could save someone a costly mistake.

chapter 4: employer & retiree coverage – stay or switch?

understanding employer and retiree coverage after 65

For many people, retirement is a clean break — a new chapter of life with new routines and, hopefully, less stress. But if you've worked for an employer that offers retiree medical benefits, or if you're still working past 65, Medicare isn't the only thing on your table. You may find yourself juggling both employer-sponsored coverage and Medicare — and trying to figure out which to keep, which to drop, and what it all means.

This chapter walks you through how employer or union retiree plans fit into the Medicare picture — and how to know if they're actually helping or quietly holding you back.

do you even have access to employer or retiree coverage?

All employer and union-sponsored coverages are considered *creditable* under Medicare rules. That means:

- ✅ You won't face late enrollment penalties for Medicare Part B or Part D as long as you maintain that coverage and transition within the allowed timeframe.
- ✅ When the coverage ends — whether due to retirement, job loss, or your spouse aging out — it triggers a **Special Enrollment Period (SEP)** that gives you time to sign up for Medicare A and B without penalty.

But here's the truth most people don't realize:

- ✅ Not everyone has access to employer or retiree coverage.
- ✅ Some employers don't offer anything at all once you leave.
- ✅ Some may offer coverage that looks great on paper but shifts costs or limits access in ways that make it less attractive once you start using it.
- ✅ And some plans — even the "free" ones — may not include spouses or dependents once you hit Medicare eligibility, causing confusion for families trying to stay together under one plan.

If you're still working and your employer offers group health coverage, that may work for now. But the moment you retire, the rules shift — and what you're offered may not look the same.

a fork in the road: stay on employer coverage or transition to medicare?

When your employer offers a retiree plan, it can feel like a gift — but it can also become a trap if you don't look closely.

Let's break down the key questions to ask when comparing your options:

✅ What does the retiree plan actually cover?
✅ Is it secondary to Medicare or primary?
✅ Does it wrap around Medicare like a Medigap plan, or does it behave more like a Medicare Advantage plan?
✅ What are the monthly costs?
✅ Some employer plans may seem "free" but include hidden copays, prescription tiers, or limited specialist networks.
✅ Others may have fixed premiums that increase yearly — often without warning.
✅ How does it compare to Medigap + Part D or a Medicare Advantage plan?
✅ Does it give you national access to doctors, or is it tied to a regional network?

☑ Are your medications covered under a flexible formulary?
☑ What happens to your spouse or dependents?

If they're under 65 and relying on your coverage, choosing to leave the employer plan may force them into an expensive COBRA plan or the individual marketplace.

Many people feel torn because the employer plan covers their spouse, but Medicare only covers them. That emotional (and financial) pressure can cloud an otherwise clear decision.

a common misconception: "it's free, so i'll just stay on it"

This comes up a lot — especially with state or municipal retiree plans that offer coverage at no monthly cost.

But let's clear something up.

Just because a plan is *free* doesn't mean it's *better*.

Here are a few trade-offs I see all the time:

☑ **Limited doctor networks** — especially for specialists or out-of-state providers.
☑ **Coordination headaches** — if Medicare is primary and the retiree plan is secondary, claims can bounce back and forth if billing isn't done correctly.
☑ **Drug coverage gaps** — some retiree plans don't include robust prescription coverage or rely on older formularies that don't match your current needs.

✅ **Locked-in restrictions** — unlike Advantage or Medigap, you can't always switch easily. Some employers only allow open enrollment once a year — or not at all once you decline.

I once had a client, a retired county employee, who proudly stayed on her free retiree plan. It wasn't until her specialist dropped out of the plan's narrow network that she realized she couldn't just switch mid-year. She had to wait months to get back on Original Medicare with a Medigap plan — and by then, she had developed a new condition that made underwriting difficult.

coordination of benefits: who pays first?

This is where things can get tricky.

If you're still actively working *and* your employer has more than 20 employees, your employer plan typically pays first, and Medicare is secondary. But if the company has fewer than 20 employees, the order flips — Medicare pays first, and the employer plan becomes secondary.

⭐ *If you're retired and receiving retiree benefits, Medicare almost always becomes the primary payer, and the retiree plan pays second — unless you're enrolled in a group-sponsored Medicare Advantage plan offered by the employer.*

This distinction matters — because if you skip enrolling in Part B when Medicare is supposed to be primary, your claims could be denied, leaving you on the hook for thousands.

group-sponsored medicare advantage plans: a different animal

Some employers now offer Medicare Advantage group plans to their retirees — and these work a bit differently than the Advantage plans you see on TV.

✅ These plans are often custom-built for the employer group.
✅ They may have better networks, lower copays, or additional benefits negotiated at the group level.
✅ But they still follow Medicare Advantage rules — meaning they replace your Medicare A and B coverage with bundled managed care.

⭐ If your employer offers one of these plans, don't assume it's your only option. You can still decline and go with Original Medicare + Medigap or another Advantage plan — but you'll need to compare coverage, doctors, and drug costs carefully.

what else you should be asking: taxes, timing, and talking to hr

As you're weighing employer or retiree coverage against Medicare, there are a few overlooked questions that can have major consequences — especially when it comes to taxes and re-enrollment timing.

Let's walk through three topics that most people don't think about until it's too late.

will employer coverage affect my taxes after 65

Once you turn 65 and become eligible for Medicare, staying on certain types of employer coverage — especially pre-tax plans like Health Savings Accounts (HSAs) — can trigger unintended tax consequences.

If you're still working and contributing to an HSA:

✅ Once you enroll in **any part of Medicare,** including Part A, you can no longer legally contribute to an HSA. If you do, you could face tax penalties and be required to reverse the contribution. This rule applies even if your employer is still offering the HSA and making contributions on your behalf.

Medicare Part A is retroactive up to 6 months:

✅ If you delay enrolling in Medicare past 65, but then enroll later (e.g., at 67 when you retire), Medicare Part A will apply retroactively for **up to six months** — as long as it doesn't go earlier than your 65th birthday. That retroactive period still disqualifies you from contributing to your HSA during that time. Many people aren't told this until tax time when it's too late to correct.

Employer contributions can still trigger penalties:

> ✅ Even if **you** stop contributing to the HSA once you enroll in Medicare, your **employer's contributions** can still create a problem. The IRS sees them the same way — and it's your responsibility to make sure they stop at the right time.

Pro Tip: If you're still working and want to delay Medicare enrollment to keep contributing to an HSA, make sure you:

> ✅ Confirm that your employer coverage is creditable for both Parts B and D
> ✅ Decline Medicare Part A (yes, this is possible — but irreversible if already accepted)
> ✅ Plan ahead and stop all HSA contributions at least **six months before** you plan to enroll in Medicare

This is where the intersection of HR policy and IRS rules gets tricky — so professional guidance is critical.

can i defer a retiree plan and pick it up later?

Some employer-sponsored retiree plans offer a one-time election: you can either take it when you retire, or walk away forever.

Others allow you to **defer** the plan, meaning you can enroll at a later date — often after trying Medicare Advantage or Medigap first.

Here's what to know:

✅ Not all retiree plans are "use it or lose it"
✅ Some large employers (especially government or union plans) allow you to defer coverage at retirement and reactivate it later. This flexibility can be a powerful safety net — but you'll need to check the fine print.
✅ Re-entry may have restrictions
✅ Just because a plan allows deferral doesn't mean it's seamless. Rejoining the plan may involve waiting periods, reapplication steps, or changes in premiums and benefits. Some plans only allow you to re-enroll during a fixed window each year, similar to employer open enrollment.
✅ You may lose dependent coverage when deferring
✅ In some plans, deferring retiree coverage means your spouse or dependent is no longer eligible — even if you return later. This can be a dealbreaker for couples trying to stay on the same plan in retirement.

⭐ **Pro Tip:** If you're considering trying Medicare first and holding your retiree plan as a backup, get written confirmation on:

☑ Whether deferral is allowed
☑ Whether dependent eligibility is retained
☑ How and when you'd be able to re-enroll
☑ Whether drug coverage through the plan meets Part D creditable coverage standards (so you avoid penalties)

The last one is critical — over the last 9 years of my career I've only witnessed this option once. Please follow up with your employer/HR department to confirm if this is a viable option.

Sample Scripts: What to Ask HR (And How to Say It)

One of the most valuable — and underused — tools in this process is your Human Resources department or retiree benefits coordinator. But most people don't know what to ask, or how to get a clear answer.

Here are three tested scripts you can use to get the information you need, without confusion:

📞 Script #1: Clarifying Enrollment Timing and Coordination

"Hi, I'm approaching age 65 and want to make sure I'm transitioning to Medicare correctly. If I stay on the employer plan for now, can you confirm when I need to enroll in Medicare Part B — and how your plan coordinates once I do? I also want to make sure I won't face any gaps or delays when I eventually switch."

Why this works:

✅ It shifts focus to Part B timing, which is where mistakes happen.
✅ It opens the door for HR to clarify how the employer plan behaves once Medicare starts — e.g., whether they become secondary, drop drug coverage, or require notice.

📞 Script #2: Understanding Retiree Plan Deferral

"I'm currently enrolled in the HSA and still working. I'd like to know when I need to stop contributions if I plan to start Medicare. Can you confirm how this works on your end — and whether the company will automatically stop contributing when I turn 65?"

Why it works:

✅ This keeps the tone respectful while surfacing two things many HR reps won't volunteer unless asked — deferral rights and spousal eligibility.

📞 Script #3: HSA + Medicare Coordination

"When I retire, I'm trying to understand what options I'll have. If I decline the retiree plan at that time, will I have the option to enroll later? And if so, will my spouse still be eligible if we come back?"

Why it works:

> ✅ This keeps the tone respectful while surfacing two things many HR reps won't volunteer unless asked — deferral rights and spousal eligibility.

wrapping up: employer coverage isn't one-size-fits-all

When it comes to employer and retiree health benefits, there's one important truth you need to know:

<u>**These plans are all private.**</u>

There's no central database, no public website, and no Medicare office that can tell you what your specific employer or union offers. Every plan is different — not just across companies, but sometimes even between divisions or retiree tiers within the same organization.

The examples and insights shared in this chapter weren't pulled from a national handbook. They've been gathered over years of real conversations with clients, helping them navigate the often confusing bridge between employer coverage and Medicare.

That's why this chapter didn't try to give you a universal answer — because there isn't one.

The goal here was simple:

✅ To help you know what questions to ask
✅ To help you avoid common coordination pitfalls
✅ And to prepare you for the kind of details that actually matter when choosing between staying on an employer plan or transitioning fully to Medicare

If you're approaching this stage, your best and most accurate source of information will always be your **Human Resources department** or **benefits administrator**. They can tell you exactly how your plan works with Medicare, what deadlines to be aware of, and what happens if you decide to defer or re-enroll in the future.

Armed with the right questions — and a clear understanding of your Medicare options — you'll be in a much stronger position to make the decision that works best for you and your family.

🇺🇸 chapter 5: va benefits, tricare & champva – military paths

va benefits & tricare with medicare — what you need to know

For many Americans, turning 65 and enrolling in Medicare is already confusing enough. But if you've served in the military or are married to someone who did, things get even more complex. You may already have access to healthcare through the **VA** or through **TRICARE**, and now Medicare is showing up at your door asking for a decision — and a premium.

That's where this chapter comes in.

Our goal here is simple:

✅ Explain how VA and TRICARE work with Medicare
✅ Show what coverage gaps may exist if you rely on just one system
✅ Help you avoid common mistakes with timing and enrollment

This is not a benefits manual. It's a real-world guide built from working with hundreds of veterans and military retirees over the years — and helping them avoid costly surprises.

if you have va benefits, do you still need medicare?

Let's start with the most common question we hear:

"If I already get all my care through the VA, do I still need Medicare?"

The short answer is: **yes, you probably do.**

Even though VA benefits can be excellent, they only cover **care received within the VA system.** That means:

✅ You must see VA-approved doctors
✅ You must go to VA hospitals and facilities
✅ You must use VA pharmacies (with limited exceptions)

The VA does not reimburse civilian doctors, clinics, or hospitals. If you need care **outside** the VA — even in an emergency — you could end up paying out of pocket unless you also have Medicare.

Let's say you're traveling out of state and need urgent care. If the nearest facility isn't a VA location, your VA benefits likely **won't cover it**. But if you have **Medicare Part A and B**, your civilian care would be covered — just like it would for any other Medicare enrollee.

That's why so many veterans choose to enroll in Medicare even if they plan to **continue using the VA for most of their care.**

Don't Forget: VA Benefits Are NOT Creditable for Part B

This is critical.

VA benefits **are** considered creditable for **Part D** (prescription drug coverage), but **they are NOT creditable for Part B** (outpatient medical coverage). That means:

- ✅ If you skip enrolling in Medicare Part B at 65 because you have VA coverage, you could face **permanent late enrollment penalties** if you decide to join later.
- ✅ You may also face **coverage gaps** if you ever need non-VA services, like a civilian specialist, hospital, or urgent care clinic.
- ✅ You cannot rely on the VA alone to meet all your healthcare needs — especially in emergencies or if your VA access changes.

There's no one-size-fits-all solution here, but skipping Medicare Part B rarely works out long term — even for veterans.

What Medicare Brings to the Table

Let's break it down.

If you have **both** VA and Medicare, you can:

✅ Use VA care when you want to
✅ Use Medicare-covered services in the civilian world
✅ Get broader access — especially for emergencies or local providers
✅ Avoid penalties if your VA access ever changes

If you only have VA benefits:

🟥 You're limited to the VA network
🟥 You're exposed to major bills if you get non-VA care
🟥 You risk facing Medicare late penalties if you try to join later

Having both systems working for you means **more flexibility**, not more complexity.

giveback plans — a medicare advantage option for veterans

In recent years, some Medicare Advantage carriers have started offering plans **specifically designed for veterans.** These are often called **giveback plans** because they give you back some or all of your **Part B premium.**

Here's how it works:

Let's say your Part B premium in 2025 is $174.70/month. A giveback plan might offer a $75 or $100 credit toward that monthly amount — paid directly into your Social Security check.

Why would a company do that?

Because these plans are **built for people who don't need full medical services from the plan.** Many veterans continue to use the VA for their doctor visits, medications, and labs. That means the Advantage plan has **lower usage**, and in turn, they pass some of those savings back to you through a giveback.

☑️ These plans still give you Medicare Advantage protection
☑️ They don't interfere with your VA care
☑️ You still pay the standard Part B premium — but the giveback offsets it

⭐ ***Important:*** *You must still* ***enroll in Medicare Parts A and B*** *to be eligible for these plans. Having VA benefits* ***does not replace Medicare enrollment.***

Real Example: How VA and Medicare Work Together

Let's say you're a 68-year-old veteran who's been using VA care exclusively for years. You rarely go to the doctor and prefer the VA pharmacy because it's affordable.

But then you have a heart issue while visiting family and need to go to the ER. The nearest VA hospital is over an hour away, so the ambulance takes you to a civilian hospital.

If you don't have Medicare:

> You may be responsible for 100% of the cost

Important: *After you've arrived at the hospital, they will inform you that you must wait for VA services to arrive to transport you to the nearest VA facility — even in an emergency.*

If you do have Medicare:

> ✅ Part A covers the hospital stay
> ✅ Part B covers any outpatient testing or doctor fees
> ✅ Your out-of-pocket is capped (especially if you also have Medigap or Advantage)

This is a **common scenario** — and one where having Medicare makes all the difference.

tricare for life: how it works with medicare

If you're a military retiree — or the spouse of one — you may already have TRICARE. But once you hit 65 and enroll in Medicare, TRICARE changes into something called **TRICARE for Life (TFL).**

For many, this setup is the gold standard of retiree healthcare. You get full access to Medicare providers, you rarely pay anything out of pocket, and your benefits stretch nationwide. But there are still important things to understand — especially around eligibility, enrollment timing, and how the two systems coordinate.

Let's break it down.

Who's Eligible for TRICARE for Life?

To qualify for TRICARE for Life, you must meet **three** key requirements:

✅ You're entitled to Medicare Part A
✅ You're enrolled in Medicare Part B
✅ You're a military retiree (or spouse/survivor) who already qualifies for TRICARE

That last one is key. TRICARE for Life is not for active-duty members or those who served a few years and left. It's reserved for **military retirees** who qualify under DEERS (Defense Enrollment Eligibility Reporting System) and are already eligible for TRICARE in general.

Once you hit 65, Medicare becomes your primary insurance — and TRICARE for Life becomes your **secondary** coverage. But unlike a civilian Medigap policy, you don't have to shop for it. It kicks in automatically as long as you're enrolled in Medicare Part B and meet eligibility.

how tricare for life coordinates with medicare

Here's where things get really smooth.

☑️ Medicare pays first for all covered services
☑️ TRICARE picks up most of the rest — including coinsurance, deductibles, and remaining balances
☑️ You rarely see a bill

This coordination is seamless for most people. As long as you see a provider who accepts Medicare, your claims are processed automatically. You don't need to file anything, and there's no need to carry multiple cards to prove you're covered.

You can use any Medicare provider, nationwide, just like someone with Medigap. And TRICARE also covers a few services Medicare does not — including overseas care, some prescription drugs, and certain extras like skilled nursing facility copays.

what you still pay with tricare for life

Even though TFL covers nearly everything, it's not completely free.

☑️ You still pay your Medicare Part B premium
☑️ You may pay small copays for prescriptions through the TRICARE pharmacy program

✅ If you get care overseas, you may need to pay up front and file for reimbursement

That said, there's no separate monthly premium for TRICARE for Life itself. Unlike Medigap or Advantage plans that charge anywhere from $50 to $300+ per month, TFL is a no-premium secondary plan. That's a huge benefit — and one of the reasons it's so valued.

How Prescription Coverage Works

This is a common area of confusion, because TFL includes its own prescription coverage — and it's not the same as Medicare Part D.

Here's how it works:

✅ If you have TRICARE for Life, you do **not** need to enroll in a separate Part D plan
✅ You get drug coverage automatically through the TRICARE pharmacy benefit
✅ You can fill prescriptions via:

- Military treatment facilities
- TRICARE Home Delivery (mail order)
- TRICARE retail pharmacy network

Costs are typically lower than civilian Part D plans, especially when using mail order or base pharmacies. And because TRICARE counts as creditable coverage for Part D, you'll never face a penalty for not enrolling in Part D later.

Pro Tip: If a civilian provider writes a prescription, make sure they're aware of your TFL status. Some pharmacies may not process it correctly unless it's coded properly.

what about foreign travel?

Medicare generally does **not** cover care received outside the United States — with only a few rare exceptions.

But TRICARE for Life **does** cover overseas care, including hospital visits and doctor services, as long as they're medically necessary.

Here's what you need to know:

✅ You may have to pay up front for care
✅ You'll need to submit a claim for reimbursement through the TRICARE Overseas Program
✅ Not all providers overseas will recognize or accept TFL — so keep records and receipts

This makes TFL one of the only plans that protects Medicare-aged travelers abroad. For military retirees who live or travel internationally, this benefit alone can be a game-changer.

why you still need medicare to use tricare for life

One common misunderstanding is thinking TRICARE for Life is a full replacement for Medicare. It's not.

You **must** have both Medicare Part A and B to use TFL. If you skip Part B to save money, you'll lose access to TFL entirely.

Let's say you turn 65, have TRICARE, but don't enroll in Medicare Part B because you don't want to pay the $174.70 monthly premium.

Here's what happens:

- Your TRICARE for Life eligibility ends
- You're now uninsured for most civilian medical services
- You may face late enrollment penalties if you try to sign up for Part B later

That's why it's critical to get your enrollment timing right. Medicare and TRICARE are a package deal — if you lose one, you lose the benefits of both working together.

---

real-world story: spouse with tfl, but no medicare

Let's look at a common situation.

Client J: He was a military retiree with TRICARE. He was covered as his spouse and assumed TRICARE would continue automatically once he turned 65.

But he never enrolled in Medicare Part B.

A few months later, he went to a civilian doctor for a basic visit. TRICARE denied the claim — because Medicare was supposed to pay first, and he wasn't enrolled.

He ended up paying the full bill out of pocket — and had to wait until the General Enrollment Period to sign up for Medicare (which only starts January 1 of each year), plus a lifetime penalty on his Part B premium.

It was an expensive lesson. TRICARE for Life **requires** you to stay compliant with Medicare rules, even if you don't use the civilian system often.

Adding a Third Layer: Why Some TRICARE for Life Members Choose a Medicare Advantage-Only Plan

This next point surprises many people — but it's becoming more and more common:

> ✅ If you have TRICARE for Life and Medicare Parts A and B, you can still enroll in a **Medicare Advantage plan** — as long as it's a **MA-only plan** (one that doesn't include drug coverage).

Why would someone do this if they already have TFL?

The most common reason is **free dental.**

TRICARE for Life and Medicare together do not include dental coverage. And while you can purchase standalone dental insurance, it often comes with waiting periods or limited networks.

Some MA-only plans offer:

✅ $0 premiums
✅ No drug plan component (so they don't interfere with your TRICARE pharmacy benefit)
✅ Included extras like:

- Preventive and comprehensive dental
- Vision and hearing benefits
- Fitness programs or OTC allowances
- May or may include a giveback to help offset Part B monthly premiums as well.

This setup gives you the best of all worlds:

✅ You keep your TFL secondary coverage
✅ You retain full Medicare Part A and B benefits
✅ You gain access to extra perks like dental — without disrupting your existing coverage

⭐ ***Important:*** *Always make sure the plan is* ***MA-only*** *— meaning it does* ***not*** *include Part D. If you enroll in a Medicare Advantage plan that includes drug coverage, it can create a conflict with your TRICARE pharmacy benefit and may even cause you to lose TFL eligibility.*

So before enrolling, double-check that:

✅ The plan has **no Part D component**
✅ It allows you to maintain all TFL protections
✅ It doesn't require referrals or limit providers you rely on through Medicare

This strategy isn't for everyone, but it's a powerful option for those who want to enhance their coverage — especially in areas like dental — without giving up the reliability of Medicare and TRICARE working together.

Common Scenarios: How VA, TRICARE, and Medicare Actually Work Together

Let's move beyond theory and into the real world. These next few stories are based on common situations I've encountered over the years — the kinds of decisions real veterans, spouses, and military retirees face every week. You'll see how different systems work together, where the traps are, and what to ask for next.

👤 Client I: A Vietnam-Era Veteran Seeking More Consistency

Client I is a 73-year-old Army veteran who had been relying on the VA system for years. He appreciated the low cost of care and trusted the VA overall — but one thing always frustrated him: the inconsistency of providers.

"At the VA, it feels like a revolving door," he told me. "Every time I go, I'm seeing a different doctor. I just want someone who knows me."

That desire for more stable, personal care is what prompted him to explore private options. Fortunately, he had enrolled in both **Medicare Part A and B** when he turned 65 — so his window was still wide open.

He came to our meeting with a goal: find a civilian doctor he could stick with long term. Before our appointment, he'd even looked up a few local providers he was interested in.

We reviewed his options and found a **Medicare Advantage giveback plan** that not only included his preferred doctor in-network but also returned $100/month toward his Part B premium.

✅ He kept his VA access for prescriptions and specialty care
✅ He gained consistency with a civilian primary doctor
✅ He pays less each month thanks to the giveback feature

Today, he tells me, "I've finally got the best of both worlds — my VA benefits, and a doctor I chose who actually knows my name."

That's what coordination looks like — not replacing one system, but blending them strategically. And because the VA and Medicare don't conflict, he's able to use both without penalty or overlap.

Client J: A Navy Retiree with TRICARE for Life — and No Idea He Needed Medicare

Client J served 22 years in the Navy. At 64, he was preparing to retire and assumed that TRICARE would just "roll over" once he hit 65.

But a year later, he called in a panic.

"I just got a bill for $1,100 from a civilian doctor," he said. "TRICARE's refusing to pay."

When we looked deeper, the issue was clear: he had never enrolled in **Medicare Part B.**

Without it, TRICARE for Life won't pay for civilian care — because Medicare is supposed to pay first. And since he skipped Part B entirely, he was now outside of his IEP and had to wait until the Special Enrollment Period, facing both a delay and a **lifetime Part B penalty.**

We helped him enroll as quickly as possible. But the missed timing cost him more than just money — it disrupted care he thought he had.

Important:

- ✅ TRICARE for Life is only active **if** you have both Medicare A and B
- ✅ Don't assume it will continue unless you follow the Medicare rules

---

Client K: Widow Navigating CHAMPVA and Medicare

Client K lost her husband — a Vietnam veteran — 10 years ago. She's now 65 and recently became eligible for Medicare.

She had CHAMPVA, which helped with civilian medical costs for years. But now, with Medicare on the table, she was confused. "Do I need both? Will one cancel the other?"

We walked through the rules:

> ✅ CHAMPVA continues as long as you enroll in both Part A and Part B
> ✅ CHAMPVA will coordinate with Medicare — similar to Medigap or TRICARE for Life
> ✅ She doesn't need a Part D plan, since CHAMPVA includes prescription coverage

She was relieved to learn that CHAMPVA wouldn't go away — but she **did** have to actively enroll in both A and B to keep it. And unlike TRICARE, there's no automatic switch to a new system at 65. She had to initiate the transition herself.

⭐ ***Important:*** *Surviving spouses with CHAMPVA must stay proactive. Medicare + CHAMPVA is a strong combo — but only if you stay enrolled correctly.*

Client L: A Veteran Without a Service-Connected Disability, But Needs More Choice

Client L served in the Marines but doesn't have a service-connected disability. That means while he's eligible for VA care, his access is limited — and he has to go through wait-lists and approvals for even basic care.

He was frustrated. "I waited three months just to get an MRI," he said. "I want more control."

He asked whether Medicare could help, and the answer was yes — but only if he enrolled in **Part B.**

He was still within his Initial Enrollment Period and chose to sign up for A and B right away. Because of that, he avoided penalties — and opened the door to:

✅ Seeing civilian doctors without VA wait times
✅ Getting tests and specialists covered through Medicare
✅ Keeping the VA as a fallback for pharmacy or specialty programs

He also opted for a **giveback plan** — a Medicare Advantage plan that reduced his Part B premium by $74.40/month. That allowed him to keep monthly costs low while gaining flexibility.

How These Scenarios Connect Back to You

Each of these clients had military service in common — but each faced a different decision. The key wasn't choosing between systems. It was knowing how to combine them smartly.

✅ VA alone may not be enough — especially in emergencies
✅ TRICARE or CHAMPVA only works **with** Medicare
✅ Medicare adds freedom — but also requires timing and strategy
✅ You can keep military care **and** use civilian options

Not Every Veteran Chooses a Giveback Plan — And That's Okay

Most of the scenarios we just walked through involve veterans enrolling in **giveback plans** — and for good reason. These plans are often designed with VA users in mind. They lower costs, provide backup coverage, and don't interfere with existing VA care.

But let me be clear: that's not the only route.

In a smaller — but still important — percentage of cases, I've worked with veterans who **intentionally chose a Medicare Advantage plan that includes drug coverage,** even though they already had access to the VA pharmacy system.

Why?

✅ Some lived far from the nearest VA facility
✅ Others didn't want to drive across town every time they needed care
✅ A few simply preferred the structure and convenience of civilian healthcare

For those clients, it wasn't about replacing their VA benefits — it was about reducing how much they had to rely on them. And since Medicare Advantage plans often include dental, vision, hearing, and extras like OTC allowances, some saw added value in that bundle.

There's no right or wrong answer here. What matters is that **you review all your options.** Just because a plan doesn't seem like a perfect fit at first glance doesn't mean it won't work well in your area. In some counties and states, the Advantage plans are far more generous than people expect — with lower MOOPs, better provider access, and rich extra benefits.

So, whoever you're working with — whether it's a broker, an agent, or just doing the research yourself — make sure they explore **all available plans**, including those you might not have considered at first. The best choice is the one that fits **your life**, not someone else's playbook.

Next Up: Enrollment Traps and Timing Mistakes to Avoid

We've now seen how VA, TRICARE, and CHAMPVA work alongside Medicare in the real world. But before we wrap this chapter up, we need to go over one last piece — the mistakes that catch people off guard.

From missed deadlines to permanent penalties, the next section will give you a simple, step-by-step roadmap to protect yourself (or a loved one) from avoidable damage.

Let's walk through the critical enrollment rules next — and how to stay protected.

enrollment traps and timing mistakes to avoid

By now, you've seen how VA, TRICARE, and CHAMPVA work with Medicare — and how different combinations can give you powerful coverage. But even with the best setup, timing is everything.

One missed enrollment window can lead to:

- ✅ Permanent late penalties
- ✅ Gaps in coverage
- ✅ Losing access to military benefits you've earned

This section walks you through the most common mistakes — and how to avoid them.

❌ Mistake #1: Assuming VA Benefits Replace Medicare

This is the single most common misunderstanding we see. Many veterans believe that because they're covered by the VA, they don't need to enroll in Medicare when they turn 65.

That's not true — and the consequences are steep.

✅ VA benefits are not considered creditable for Part B
✅ If you delay Medicare Part B without having employer coverage, you'll face a **10% late enrollment penalty** for every 12-month period you go without it
✅ That penalty is permanent — for life

Even worse, if you later decide to get civilian care and try to enroll in Part B, you may have to wait for the next available enrollment period; Annual Enrollment Period (Oct. 15th to Dec 7th, your plan won't be effective until the following year) Open Enrollment Period (Jan 1st – March 31st.) Special Election Period (March 31st – Oct 14th) That means the coverage gap can vary depending on the month you are currently in.

***Important:** If you're turning 65 and only have VA coverage — enroll in both Medicare Part A and B during your **Initial Enrollment Period (IEP)** to avoid penalties and delays.*

❌ Mistake #2: Thinking TRICARE for Life Works Without Medicare

TRICARE for Life (TFL) is an incredible benefit — but it only works **after** you enroll in Medicare Parts A and B.

If you skip Medicare, you lose TRICARE completely.

There's no partial coverage. No forgiveness. No appeal.

- ✅ TFL becomes your secondary coverage once you have A and B
- ✅ If you don't enroll in Medicare when you're supposed to, TRICARE will drop you until you fix it
- ✅ And once again, you may be stuck waiting for the next enrollment window — with no coverage in the meantime

⭐ ***Important:*** *If you have TRICARE and are turning 65, mark your calendar. Your IEP begins three months before your 65th birthday and ends three months after. If you don't enroll in time, you risk losing access to TRICARE for Life.*

❌ Mistake #3: Enrolling in the Wrong Type of Medicare Advantage Plan

If you're a veteran with VA or TRICARE and you want to explore Medicare Advantage, it's critical to choose the right kind of plan.

- ✅ If you have VA or TRICARE, and you're only looking to supplement with civilian benefits like dental or hearing, look for **MA-only plans** (without drug coverage). These can include giveback options and often provide extras without conflicting with your military benefits.
- ✅ If you enroll in a **Medicare Advantage plan that includes Part D**, you could accidentally override your VA or TRICARE drug coverage. This might cause coordination problems or even disqualify you from continuing your military pharmacy benefits in some cases.

📌 ***Important:*** *Always confirm the type of Advantage plan before enrolling. And if you're working with an agent, make sure they know you have VA, TRICARE, or CHAMPVA before showing you plan options.*

❌ Mistake #4: Missing Giveback Plan Opportunities

Some veterans enroll in standard Medicare Advantage plans and overlook giveback options — which could be putting money back in their pocket every month.

- ✅ If you're enrolled in Medicare Parts A and B, and not using civilian healthcare services through Medicare, a giveback plan can help offset your $174.70 monthly Part B premium
- ✅ These plans don't interfere with VA care

- ✅ Many come with added perks — dental, vision, hearing — which the VA doesn't always provide

But they're not available in every area. And not every agent will mention them — especially if they're not familiar with how they interact with VA benefits.

***Important:** When shopping for plans, specifically ask about **giveback Medicare Advantage plans designed for veterans.** Even if you don't plan to use them for your main care, they can reduce your overall costs and add flexibility.*

---

key enrollment periods to know

To avoid penalties and gaps, you need to understand the major enrollment windows tied to military and Medicare benefits.

- ✅ **Initial Enrollment Period (IEP):**
Your seven-month window when you first become eligible for Medicare — three months before, your birthday month, and three months after.
- ✅ **Special Enrollment Period (SEP) — Employer Coverage Ends:**
*If you're still working past 65 and covered by employer insurance, you get an SEP when that coverage ends. You have **eight months** from the time your employer coverage stops to enroll in Part B — without penalty.*
- ✅ **General Enrollment Period (GEP):**

If you miss your IEP and don't qualify for a SEP, you can only enroll in Medicare Part B during the GEP: January 1 through March 31. But coverage won't start until July — and you'll face penalties if you waited too long.
✅ **CHAMPVA Eligibility Triggers:**
CHAMPVA requires both Parts A and B — just like TRICARE. If you skip Part B, you lose access to CHAMPVA. There are no exceptions.

don't forget: you can't just "fix it later"

Many people assume that if they make a mistake during enrollment — or skip something now — they can just "fix it" later.

But Medicare doesn't always work that way – it can but at what cost?

✅ Penalties for late enrollment are permanent
✅ Certain benefits (like TRICARE or CHAMPVA) may be suspended if you skip Medicare Parts A and B
✅ Enrollment windows are strict, and if you miss them, you may wait months before coverage begins

And in the meantime, if something happens — a hospital stay, a new diagnosis, an emergency — you may have no coverage and no backup plan.

how to protect yourself (or a loved one)

If you're a veteran, military retiree, or the spouse of someone who served, here are a few smart moves you can make today:

✅ Make a list of every type of coverage you currently have — VA, TRICARE, employer, or other
✅ Write down your 65th birthday (or your spouse's) and count back three months — that's when you should start planning
✅ Check with your local VA office or TRICARE contact center to confirm how your military benefits interact with Medicare
✅ Don't assume your agent or broker understands the VA system — always ask specific questions

And most importantly:

Don't let confusion delay your decision. Medicare timelines are not forgiving, and your military benefits depend on getting this right the first time.

wrapping it up: what military families need to know

Serving in the military means you've earned access to some of the strongest benefits available — but when Medicare enters the picture, the path forward can still feel confusing. You're not alone in that.

What this chapter has hopefully made clear is that Medicare and military benefits don't have to conflict. In fact, when structured correctly, they often complement one another in powerful ways.

Here's a quick recap of the most important takeaways:

✅ **VA benefits work well — but only inside the VA system.**
That means no civilian doctors, no outside hospitals, and no private pharmacy coverage unless you also have Medicare. Enrolling in Part B ensures you can get care outside the VA when needed.
✅ **TRICARE for Life acts like a built-in Medigap plan.**
Once you have both Parts A and B, TRICARE steps in as your secondary — covering many of the out-of-pocket costs that would otherwise fall on you. It also includes prescription coverage, so you don't need a separate Part D plan.
✅ **You must enroll in Medicare at the right time.**
Don't assume military coverage delays or replaces the need for Medicare. Missing your IEP can result in permanent penalties and cause you to lose access to benefits like TRICARE or CHAMPVA.
✅ **Giveback Advantage plans can be a smart add-on.**
Especially for VA users, a $0-premium Advantage plan that gives back part of the Part B premium — and offers dental or vision — can be a great way to get more without paying more. Just be sure to avoid drug-inclusive plans if you already use VA or TRICARE for prescriptions.

final thoughts: you've earned this — now protect it

It's easy to feel like you need a law degree to read through your TRICARE handbook or VA enrollment guide. Add Medicare on top of that, and the entire process can feel overwhelming.

But you don't have to become an expert overnight.

You just need to understand the key intersections:

✅ When to enroll
✅ What parts of Medicare you need
✅ How your military coverage fits in
✅ What your options are if you want extras — like dental, vision, or civilian access

If you're unsure, your best bet is to speak with someone who understands both the Medicare and military systems. Whether it's a certified Medicare advisor, a SHIP counselor, or a benefits officer at the VA or TRICARE office — don't be afraid to ask questions.

📞 You can also call Medicare directly at 1-800-MEDICARE, or TRICARE for Life at 1-866-773-0404 for clarification.

what to ask before making a decision

Before you lock in your Medicare path, here are some simple but powerful questions to ask yourself — or your representative:

✅ Am I currently using the VA or TRICARE as my primary care source?
✅ Do I want the freedom to see doctors outside the military system if needed?
✅ Have I confirmed whether I'm required to enroll in Part B to keep my benefits?
✅ Would a giveback plan or MA-only plan provide added value without causing conflict?
✅ Do I need dental, vision, or hearing coverage that my current military plan doesn't offer?
✅ Do I have a list of all enrollment deadlines that apply to me?

These aren't hypothetical — they're the exact questions I've used in real-life client conversations. And they work.

For Spouses and Family Members

A quick word for those of you helping a spouse or parent:

Your support matters more than you realize. Medicare planning is already emotional — and adding military history, VA paperwork, or TRICARE complexity can make things feel even heavier.

Stay patient. Be kind. And remember that your loved one may be struggling to accept changes in their care, their independence, or their identity.

Help them organize. Call the VA or TRICARE office together. Write down questions before your appointments.

The system may be complicated — but your role in navigating it is one of the most meaningful things you can do.

closing this chapter

You've served. You've earned these benefits. Now it's time to put them to work — in the way that fits your life, your needs, and your goals.

Medicare isn't trying to replace your VA or TRICARE benefits. It's there to support you when those systems fall short — whether that's in an emergency, across state lines, or for services you can't access easily through the military.

This chapter wasn't about telling you what to do. It was about making sure you have the knowledge to do it confidently.

Let's move forward — toward coverage that truly honors your service and supports your next chapter in life.

🚀 chapter 6: what to do next

what to do next

You've made it through a maze that most people never truly figure out. You've asked hard questions, looked past the marketing, and taken time to understand a system that was never built to be simple. If you're feeling a little overwhelmed — that's normal. But if you're also feeling more prepared than you were at the start of this book, then you've already won.

This chapter isn't about new facts or charts. It's about helping you take everything you've learned and turn it into a clear next step.

Because the truth is, most Medicare mistakes don't come from picking the "wrong" plan — they come from waiting too long, trusting the wrong source, or being too afraid to act. That won't be you.

Let's finish this strong — with clarity, not confusion.

the hardest part is over

Deciding how to handle your Medicare coverage isn't just a financial or medical decision. It's emotional.

For some people, it brings up fears about aging, or frustration that things aren't clearer. Others feel pressure from adult children, spouses, or even former employers who mean well — but aren't in your shoes.

If that's you, know this: You're not doing anything wrong by feeling the weight of this choice.

But also know that Medicare isn't a one-shot deal. It's a system with built-in windows, protections, and flexibility. Yes, some rules are strict. But the system also gives you chances to reassess and switch when life changes — and it will.

So, take a breath. You've already done more than most people ever do by reading this book. You don't need perfection. You just need a path forward that makes sense for where you are now.

from overwhelm to action

Here's a simple mental shift that helps:

Instead of asking yourself,

"What's the best plan out there?"

Try asking:

"What's the right path for me *right now* based on how I actually use care, my current budget, and what kind of experience I want?"

That question invites clarity. It cuts through fear. And it gives you room to make an honest, human decision.

Even better? You can revisit it next year. Or the year after that. Medicare isn't static — and neither are you.

Many of the clients I work with shift plans over time. Healthy 65-year-olds often start on Medicare Advantage, then switch to Medigap if their needs change. Others begin with Medigap for security and switch later to save on premiums. There is no shame in changing direction.

So, forget the idea that there's only one "correct" answer. There's only what's right for you — today.

> ✅ **Who Can Actually Help You (and Who Can't)**
> There's no shortage of people offering Medicare advice. But here's the difference between helpful and harmful:

Helpful Sources:

> ✅ **SHIP (State Health Insurance Assistance Programs)**
> *Free, unbiased help — available in every state. Perfect if you want to speak with someone who isn't selling anything.*

☑️ **Licensed Medicare-Focused Brokers**
A good broker can simplify your options, explain plan differences in plain English, and help you enroll. Many work with all the major carriers. Just be sure to ask if they represent all plan types (Medigap and Advantage).
☑️ **Veteran or TRICARE Benefit Coordinators**
If you're a veteran, these professionals can help you understand how your military benefits interact with Medicare — and guide you toward plans that won't conflict.
☑️ **Your State's Department on Aging**
They often offer local counseling resources and workshops for new Medicare enrollees.

Less Helpful (and sometimes risky):

🚫 **Cold Callers**
If someone calls out of the blue promising "free benefits," hang up. This is how scams start — and how people accidentally enroll in plans that aren't right for them.
🚫 **One-Size-Fits-All Agents**
Some agents only sell Medicare Advantage. Others only push one company. Always ask how many carriers they work with — and whether they're allowed to sell both Medigap and Advantage. If not, you're only seeing half the picture.
🚫 **Well-Meaning Friends or Family**
A plan that works great for your cousin in Florida might be a disaster for you in New Jersey. Accept their advice with grace — and then get your own answers.

questions to ask before you enroll

No matter which path you're considering, here are the core questions I walk through with every client. Think of this as your Medicare "cheat sheet."

✅ Do all my doctors — including specialists — accept this plan?
✅ What will I owe if I have surgery, rehab, or a hospital stay?
✅ Is prior authorization required for important procedures?
✅ How are my medications covered — and are they in-network pharmacies nearby?
✅ What happens if I move or travel for extended periods?
✅ Is this a plan I can stick with, or will I want to reassess next year?

You can bring this list to any phone call, broker meeting, or plan appointment. It's not about sounding smart — it's about protecting yourself.

what comes next

Let's shift from theory to action. In the next part of this chapter, we'll give you a simple checklist — one that covers everything you need to finalize your Medicare setup and feel good about your choice.

You'll also get a few closing thoughts — not just as a Medicare learner, but as a person navigating an important life transition.

The finish line is close. And you're more prepared than you think.

Final Checklist: Your Medicare Setup, Simplified

This checklist isn't meant to overwhelm you — it's designed to help you pause, double-check a few key areas, and feel confident in your next steps. Whether you're brand new to Medicare or reevaluating your current setup, these are the questions that matter most.

Medicare Basics

✅ Have you enrolled in Medicare Part A and B — or do you know when you plan to?
✅ If you delayed Part B due to employer coverage, do you understand your SEP (Special Enrollment Period) window and deadlines?
✅ Do you know whether your current coverage is considered **creditable** for Part B and Part D?

⭐ **Remember: Employer coverage is always considered creditable.**

But **VA coverage is only creditable for Part D** — not Part B. That distinction matters.

Coverage Decision

✅ Have you decided whether to go with Medicare Advantage or Original Medicare + Medigap + Part D?
✅ Do you understand the pros and cons of both models — including networks, referrals, costs, and provider access?
✅ Have you compared the actual costs for how *you* use care (not just the monthly premium)?

Drug Coverage

✅ If you're going with a Medigap + Part D route, have you selected a Part D plan that matches your medications?
✅ If you're using the VA or TRICARE for prescriptions, do you know whether you can skip Part D without penalty?

Coverage Gaps and Protection

✅ Do you understand what your plan covers — and what it doesn't?
✅ Have you reviewed your plan's out-of-pocket maximum (MOOP)?
✅ If you're using VA or TRICARE, do you know what happens in an emergency or out-of-network situation?

Communication and Confidence

- ✅ Have you spoken with a licensed broker, SHIP counselor, or plan representative — someone who can walk you through the fine print?
- ✅ Have you clarified coverage with your HR department if you're still working or retiring soon?
- ✅ Have you written down your Medicare ID, policy numbers, and plan contact info in one place?
- ✅ Do you have someone — a family member, friend, or caregiver — who knows your setup in case of emergency?

Avoiding Future Surprises

You've made your choice. You've done the legwork. Now the goal is to stay protected — and not get caught off guard when life changes.

Here are a few habits that help:

- ✅ **Mark your calendar** for review points. Even if you're happy with your plan, mark October 1 (start of the Annual Enrollment preview) and October 15 (start of the enrollment window) every year. That way, you're never scrambling or missing out.
- ✅ **Check your Annual Notice of Change (ANOC)** each fall. Your plan may change premiums, doctor networks, copays, or drug coverage. This letter usually arrives in September. Read it.
- ✅ **Keep an eye on new benefits.** Some Advantage plans add dental, OTC allowances, givebacks, or

broader coverage each year. Don't assume your plan is still the best one — review your options, even if you stay put.

✅ **Ask about your state's extra help programs.** Many readers qualify for financial assistance (like LIS, QMB, or MSPs) and don't even realize it. These programs can dramatically lower your drug costs, premiums, or out-of-pocket limits.

✅ **If your health changes — revisit your plan.** You're allowed to reassess each year. Medicare isn't "one and done." It's a system that expects you to adjust over time.

closing thoughts: you've got this

If you've read this far, you've already done something powerful: You've taken control of your healthcare future.

Most people never do. They guess. They rush. They delay. And sometimes, they pay the price — in penalties, coverage gaps, or unnecessary stress.

But not you.

You've shown that you're willing to ask better questions. That you're not here to blindly follow advice or get talked into a plan that doesn't fit. That you're willing to think strategically about what kind of care, support, and financial protection you want — now and later.

That matters.

This book wasn't meant to make you a Medicare expert. It was meant to make you confident enough to say:

"I may not know everything — but I know what questions to ask. And I know what matters most to me."

That's what real power looks like.

Whether you're choosing for yourself, helping a spouse, or supporting an aging parent — you now have something most people never get in this system: **clarity.**

And clarity is how we protect our time, our money, and our peace of mind.

What's Next?

Here's what I recommend:

✅ **Review your checklist.** Make sure you've answered all the questions that apply to you.
✅ **Contact a licensed expert.** Preferably one who works with all carriers and plans — and who listens first, sells second.
✅ **Give yourself credit.** You just made one of the most complicated parts of retirement a whole lot simpler.

If you need to refer back to anything, go to the Appendix. There's a glossary, a one-page comparison chart, and a simple worksheet to walk you through these steps again.

No matter what path you choose — Medigap or Advantage, VA or TRICARE, employer coverage or none at all — just remember this:

You don't have to know it all.

You just have to ask the right questions and stay curious.

And now, you do.

To help you go even further, we've included a few tools in the back of this book — starting with a plain-English glossary and real-world plan comparison sheet.

📎 appendix

1. Glossary of Terms (Plain English) 📖

This glossary is designed to help you quickly understand key Medicare-related terms without needing to wade through legal or bureaucratic language. Keep it handy as you explore your coverage options.

Medicare Part A (Hospital Stays)

Hospital insurance. Covers inpatient stays, skilled nursing facility care, hospice, and some home health care.

Medicare Part B (Doctor Services)

Medical insurance. Covers doctor visits, outpatient services, preventive care, and durable medical equipment. Monthly premium applies.

Medicare Part C (Medicare Advantage)

An alternative to Original Medicare offered by private insurance companies. Bundles Part A, Part B, and often Part D (drug coverage), plus extra benefits like dental or vision.

Medicare Part D (Prescription Drug Coverage)

Prescription drug coverage. Offered through private plans that either stand alone or are bundled with Medicare Advantage.

Medigap (Medicare Supplement)

A private insurance policy that helps cover out-of-pocket costs not paid by Original Medicare (like copays and coinsurance). Sold separately from Medicare.

Maximum Out-of-Pocket (MOOP)

The most you'll spend in a year on covered medical services under a Medicare Advantage plan. After you reach this amount, the plan pays 100%.

Giveback Plan

A type of Medicare Advantage plan that returns part of your Part B premium back to you, often used by veterans who get most of their care through the VA. ***Important:*** *not limited to veterans only, civilians have access as well*

TRICARE for Life (TFL)

Military retiree coverage that works as a secondary payer to Medicare. Requires enrollment in both Medicare Part A and Part B.

CHAMPVA

Coverage for certain spouses, widows, or dependents of disabled or deceased veterans. Like TFL, requires both Medicare Parts A and B to remain active.

Creditable Coverage

Health insurance that's considered as good as (or better than) Medicare. Needed to avoid late enrollment penalties. ⭐ ***Important:*** *Employer plans are creditable. VA is only creditable for Part D.*

Late Enrollment Penalty

A permanent monthly fee added to your Medicare premium if you delay signing up for Part B or Part D without creditable coverage.

Enrollment Periods:

The windows of time when you can sign up for Medicare or make plan changes:

- ✅ **IEP (Initial Enrollment Period):** The 7-month window around your 65th birthday
- ✅ **SEP (Special Enrollment Period):** Triggered by events like losing employer coverage
- ✅ **AEP (Annual Election Period):** October 15 – December 7; change Advantage or Part D plans
- ✅ **OEP (Open Enrollment Period):** January 1 – March 31; switch Medicare Advantage plans

Formulary

The list of drugs a Part D or Advantage plan covers. Plans vary widely — always check your medications.

Network

A group of doctors, hospitals, or providers that contract with a specific Medicare Advantage plan. Staying in-network usually means lower costs.

Prior Authorization

A requirement to get approval from your plan before receiving certain services or medications. Common with Medicare Advantage plans.

Trial Right

A special protection allowing you to try a Medicare Advantage plan and return to Medigap within 12 months — ***Important:** only if you came from Medigap originally, and must return to the same company and plan letter.*

Skilled Nursing Facility (SNF)

A rehab or recovery center where you get medical care after a hospital stay. Medicare covers up to 100 days under specific conditions.

Durable Medical Equipment (DME)

Medical tools like walkers, oxygen tanks, or diabetic monitors that are covered under Part B.

Out-of-Pocket Costs

What you pay directly — including copays, coinsurance, and deductibles. These vary greatly between Medigap and Advantage.

2. Plan Comparison Quick Sheet 📊

📌 *A side-by-side look at how Medigap + Part D and Medicare Advantage stack up — in plain language.*

This sheet is designed to help you quickly compare the two most common Medicare paths. It's not about which one is "better" — it's about understanding which one fits your needs and lifestyle.

Feature	Medigap + Part D	Medicare Advantage (Part C)
Doctor Choice	✅ See any provider that accepts Medicare	✅ Must use plan's network (unless PPO)
Referrals Needed	✅ No referrals required	✅ Usually no referrals in 2025, but rare exceptions may apply
Prescription Drugs	🚫 Not included — must add a Part D plan	✅ Usually included
Monthly Premiums	💵 Higher (Plan G average: $160/month) + Part D (~$20)	💵 Many $0 premium options
Out-of-Pocket Costs	✅ Predictable — very little beyond monthly premium	💡 Copays, coinsurance, MOOP applies
Max Out-of-Pocket (MOOP)	🚫 No MOOP — costs covered after deductible	✅ MOOP limit (avg. $7,550–$14,000 in 2025)
Dental, Vision, Hearing	🚫 Not included	✅ Often included
Extra Benefits	🚫 Not typical	✅ OTC card, gym, transportation, etc.
Part B Giveback	🚫 Not applicable	✅ Some plans offer up to $175/month back
Emergency Coverage Nationwide	✅ Covered anywhere in the U.S.	✅ Covered, but out-of-network costs may apply
Best For	✅ People who want freedom, stability, and nationwide access	✅ People who want simplicity, low premiums, and extras
Worst Fit For	❌ People who rarely use care and want extras	❌ People with complex conditions who dislike networks or restrictions

⭐ Important Notes:

✅ **Both** options require enrollment in **Medicare Part A and B.**
✅ You cannot be enrolled in **both Medigap and Medicare Advantage at the same time.**
✅ Choosing the right path depends on your **health-**

care usage, budget, provider preferences, and comfort with managed care.

---

3. New Jersey Plan Highlights (2025) 🔍

Using the 2025 UnitedHealthcare® Summary of Benefits as a Real-World Example

This section walks you through how to read and understand a real Medicare Advantage plan — using the 2025 UnitedHealthcare plan offered widely across New Jersey counties. This is one of the most commonly offered $0-premium PPO plans for people **without Medicaid, LIS, or other financial assistance.**

We'll highlight what to look for when reviewing a Summary of Benefits, and how to compare those details to your needs.

What to Look for in a Summary of Benefits:

When reviewing any Medicare Advantage plan, here are the most important sections to focus on:

Monthly Premium

> ✅ This plan has a **$0 monthly premium**, which is common for base-level PPO options in New Jersey.
> ✅ You must still pay the **Part B premium ($174.70 in 2025)**. This amount is not something you pay for manually, prior to receiving your monthly Social Security Checks, it will be deducted automatically. You will receive the difference.

Doctor Visits

- ☑ **Primary Care:** $0 per visit
- ☑ **Specialist:** $40 per visit
- ☑ **Be** sure your preferred doctors are *in-network*. For PPOs, you can see out-of-network providers, but the cost may be higher.

Outpatient Services

- ☑ **Lab services:** $0
- ☑ **Outpatient X-rays:** $15–$75
- ☑ **Ambulatory surgery center:** $295 per visit
- ☑ **Review** this section carefully if you have scheduled procedures or ongoing treatments.

Hospital Coverage

- ☑ **Inpatient hospital care:** $310 per day (days 1–6), then $0
- ☑ **This** could result in over $1,800 for a single hospital stay — check the plan's MOOP (below).

Maximum Out-of-Pocket (MOOP)

- ☑ **In-Network:** $7,550
- ☑ **Combined In/Out-of-Network:** $11,300
- ☑ **This** is your financial safety net. Once you reach this number in covered services, the plan pays 100% for the rest of the year.

Prescription Drug Coverage (Part D)

✅ **Deductible:** $545 (applies only to Tiers 3, 4, 5)
✅ **Copays:**

- Tier 1 (Preferred Generic): $0
- Tier 2 (Generic): $5
- Tier 3 (Preferred Brand): $42
- Tier 4 (Non-Preferred): $100
- Tier 5 (Specialty): 33% coinsurance

📌 Be sure to check your medications against the plan's formulary. Tier placement affects your monthly costs significantly.

Extra Benefits

✅ **Dental:** Preventive and comprehensive dental services included
✅ **Vision & Hearing:** Eye exams, lenses, and hearing aids covered
✅ **OTC Credit:** $100 per quarter for over-the-counter items
✅ **Fitness Program:** Free gym access through Renew Active

📌 These extras add value — but make sure they're benefits you'll actually use.

How to Compare It to Other Plans

When evaluating a plan like this, compare:

✅ Your providers: Are your doctors in-network?
✅ Your prescriptions: Are your medications covered affordably?
✅ Your expected care needs: Will you need surgery, rehab, frequent tests?
✅ Your preference for structure vs. flexibility: Are you okay with copays and rules, or do you prefer predictability?

Tip: Use a Simple Comparison Grid

Feature	UHC PPO Plan (2025)	Medigap Plan G + Part D
Monthly Premium	$0	~$180–$200
Specialist Copay	$40	$0
MOOP	$7,550	None (covers 100% after deductible)
Drug Deductible	$545 (Tier 3+)	Varies by Part D plan
Dental/Vision/Hearing	Included	Not included
OTC Card	$100/quarter	Not included

---

4. Enrollment Timeline & Key Dates 📆

Protect Yourself from Penalties, Gaps, and Missed Opportunities

One of the most confusing parts of Medicare is knowing **when** you're supposed to act. People often miss critical deadlines — not because they're careless, but because no one told them how Medicare's timelines actually work.

This section gives you a clear breakdown of the **most important enrollment windows**, what they mean, and who they apply to. Keep this list handy — or better yet, mark your calendar.

Key Medicare Enrollment Periods:

Initial Enrollment Period (IEP)

✅ **Who it's for:** People turning 65
✅ **When it happens:** Starts 3 months before your 65th birthday month and ends 3 months after (7-month window)
✅ **What you can do:** Enroll in Part A and B, and choose a Medicare Advantage plan or Medigap + Part D combo

⭐ **Important:** If you're already receiving Social Security, enrollment into A and B may happen automatically — but Part D or Advantage still requires action.

General Enrollment Period (GEP)

✅ **Who it's for:** People who missed their IEP and aren't eligible for a Special Enrollment Period
✅ **When it happens:** January 1 to March 31 each year
✅ **What you can do:** Enroll in Part A and/or B — coverage begins July 1

⭐ **Important:** You may face late penalties, especially for Part B.

Special Enrollment Periods (SEPs)

✅ **Who it's for:** People losing employer coverage or qualifying for other life events
✅ **When it happens:** Depends on your situation (e.g., 8 months after losing employer insurance)
✅ **What you can do:** Enroll in Part A and B without penalty; choose Advantage or Part D

⭐ **Important:** Retirement, moving out of a plan's service area, losing Medicaid or Extra Help

Annual Enrollment Period (AEP)

✅ **Who it's for:** Anyone already enrolled in Medicare
✅ **When it happens:** October 15 to December 7
✅ **What you can do:** Switch Advantage plans, drop Advantage and return to Original Medicare, or change your Part D plan
✅ **Effective date:** Changes take effect January 1 of the next year

Medicare Advantage Open Enrollment Period (MA OEP)

✅ **Who it's for:** People already enrolled in a Medicare Advantage plan
✅ **When it happens:** January 1 to March 31
✅ **What you can do:** Make a **one-time** switch to a different Advantage plan or return to Original Medicare + Part D

📌 **Important:** You cannot use this period to enroll in Advantage if you weren't already in one

Part D Late Enrollment Penalty

✅ You must have **creditable drug coverage** (like from an employer, VA, or Part D plan)
✅ If you go **63+ days without** creditable drug coverage after eligibility, you'll pay a **lifetime penalty**
✅ This penalty is **added to your Part D premium** permanently

Part B Late Enrollment Penalty

✅ If you delay enrolling in Part B **without creditable employer coverage**, you face a **10% penalty for every 12-month period delayed**
✅ This penalty is also permanent and added to your monthly Part B premium

🔔 **Reminders to Set Now**

✅ 3 Months Before Age 65 — Start researching plans and confirm if you'll need to enroll manually
✅ 6 Months After Employer Coverage Ends — Make sure you're enrolled in both Part A and B to avoid late penalties
✅ Every September — Review your current plan (Advantage or Part D) before AEP begins
✅ Every January — If you're in Medicare Advantage,

evaluate whether you're happy with the plan during MA OEP

---

5. State & Federal Resources 🏛

Where to Get Trusted Help — Without the Sales Pitch

Even with the clearest guide, Medicare decisions can still feel overwhelming. Whether you want someone to walk you through your options, check plan availability in your zip code, or answer specific coverage questions, there are free and reputable resources available.

Below is a curated list of trusted **federal, state, and non-profit** support options — including some tailored for readers in New Jersey.

National Medicare Help:

1-800-MEDICARE (1-800-633-4227)

✅ Available 24/7
✅ Official Medicare call center
✅ Can help you compare plans, check coverage, and file complaints
✅ TTY: 1-877-486-2048

Medicare.gov

✅ The official Medicare website
✅ Use the "Plan Finder" tool to compare Medicare Advantage, Part D, and Medigap options
✅ Access your personal Medicare account, claims, and enrollment status

Social Security Administration (SSA.gov or 1-800-772-1213)

✅ Handles enrollment into Medicare Part A and B
✅ Can also help with LIS (Extra Help) and low-income premium assistance
✅ Local offices available in every state

State-Level Support (New Jersey):

NJ SHIP (State Health Insurance Assistance Program)

✅ Free, unbiased counseling for Medicare beneficiaries
✅ Trained volunteers provide one-on-one help with choosing and understanding plans
✅ Website: www.state.nj.us/humanservices/doas/services/ship
✅ Phone: 1-800-792-8820

NJ Save

✅ Online application for low-income seniors seeking assistance with Medicare premiums, prescription costs, and other health-related expenses

✅ Helps determine eligibility for programs like SLMB, QMB, and PAAD

✅ Website: www.nj.gov/njsave

PAAD (Pharmaceutical Assistance to the Aged and Disabled)

✅ Helps eligible NJ residents with prescription drug costs

✅ Coordinates with Part D and may reduce out-of-pocket drug expenses

✅ Toll-free: 1-800-792-9745

✅ Website: www.state.nj.us/humanservices/doas/services/paad

Veteran & Military Resources:

VA Health Benefits (1-877-222-VETS)

✅ For veterans seeking information on VA care and how it interacts with Medicare

✅ Website: www.va.gov/health-care

TRICARE for Life

✅ Medicare-coordinated coverage for military retirees

✅ Website: www.tricare.mil/tfl

✅ Phone: 1-866-773-0404

CHAMPVA Program

✅ Health coverage for spouses or survivors of disabled or deceased veterans
✅ Website: www.va.gov/health-care/family-care giver-benefits/champva
✅ Phone: 1-800-733-8387

Other Helpful Tools

Medigap Rate Comparison Tool (Medicare.gov)

✅ See Medigap plan prices side-by-side in your area
✅ Go to: www.medicare.gov/medigap-supplemental-insurance-plans

Plan Finder Tool (Medicare.gov)

✅ Enter your zip code, medications, and doctors to see plan costs and coverage
✅ Use this every year during AEP to shop Advantage and Part D plans

These resources exist to **support you — not sell you.** If you're ever unsure where to start, SHIP and Medicare.gov are two of the safest bets.

That completes the Appendix.

This book was written to give you real, honest guidance — not just facts. If you've read this far, you now have a clearer path through one of the most confusing systems in healthcare.

You're not just prepared — you're ahead of the curve.

Coming Soon: In my next series of books, I'll be covering state-specific programs that help enhance your existing Medicare coverage — no matter which path you've chosen. Each guide will focus on one state at a time, offering practical, easy-to-understand support. Stay tuned!

references

1. **Centers for Medicare & Medicaid Services (CMS)**
    - *Medicare & You 2025 Handbook*
    - https://www.medicare.gov
    - Source for Medicare rules, coverage limits, enrollment periods, and Part A/B definitions.
2. **Social Security Administration (SSA)**
    - *Medicare Enrollment and Premium Details*
    - https://www.ssa.gov/benefits/medicare/
    - Used to explain the Part B premium, IRMAA adjustments, and Social Security integration.
3. **U.S. Department of Veterans Affairs (VA)**
    - *Health Benefits Overview*
    - https://www.va.gov/health-care/about-va-health-benefits/
    - Used to describe VA eligibility, access restrictions, and coordination with Medicare.
4. **TRICARE (Defense Health Agency)**
    - *TRICARE for Life Handbook* (2025 Edition)
    - https://tricare.mil
    - Used for TRICARE and CHAMPVA coordination rules with Medicare Parts A and B.
5. **New Jersey Department of Human Services – Division of Aging Services**
    - *SHIP (State Health Insurance Assistance Program)*
    - https://www.state.nj.us/humanservices/doas/services/ship/
    - Resource recommended in Chapter 6 for unbiased local plan guidance.
6. **Clover Health – 2025 Summary of Benefits (New Jersey PPO Plan)**
    - Official Summary of Benefits Document (used for real-world Advantage examples)
    - Access via https://www.cloverhealth.com

7. **UnitedHealthcare (AARP) – 2025 Medicare Advantage Plan Summary**
   - Used in Chapter 2 and Appendix to explain structure and plan details
   - https://www.uhc.com/medicare
8. **Medigap Plan Standardization Chart – CMS**
   - *2025 Medigap Coverage Comparison Tool*
   - Available at https://www.medicare.gov/supplements-other-insurance/how-to-compare-medigap-policies
9. **Medicare Rights Center**
   - *Educational Tools and FAQs*
   - https://www.medicarerights.org
   - Used for common enrollment mistake examples and appeals support.
10. **Real-World Case Experience**

- *All client stories and case studies in this book are based on real interactions compiled by the author across more than 9 years of experience. Details have been anonymized or adjusted to protect privacy.*

www.ingramcontent.com/pod-product-compliance
Lightning Source LLC
LaVergne TN
LVHW022049200926
848481LV00003B/843